Editor
Erica N. Russikoff, M.A.

Editor in Chief
Karen J. Goldfluss, M.S. Ed.

Creative Director
Sarah M. Fournier

Cover Artist
Barb Lorseyedi

Imaging
Craig Gunnell

Publisher
Mary D. Smith, M.S. Ed.

TCR 3896

Nonfiction & Fiction PAIRED TEXTS

- Contains fiction and nonfiction passages on a variety of topics
- Includes critical-thinking questions to improve comprehension
- Extends the reading by using interactive writing activities
- Correlated to the Common Core State Standards

Teacher Created Resources

Author

Susan Mackey Collins, M. Ed.

CORRELATED TO COMMON CORE STANDARDS

For correlations to the Common Core State Standards, see pages 143–144. Correlations can also be found at *http://www.teachercreated.com/standards.*

Teacher Created Resources
6421 Industry Way
Westminster, CA 92683
www.teachercreated.com

ISBN: 978-1-4206-3896-7

© 2015 Teacher Created Resources
Made in U.S.A.

Teacher Created Resources

Table of Contents

Table of Contents (cont.)

Introduction

Making connections is an important part of everyday life. People strive daily to make connections with other people, events, and experiences. Making connections plays an important role in nearly everything one does. It is not surprising then that this skill must also be used in developing great readers.

Connections are vital in developing fluency in reading and in understanding a variety of texts. *Nonfiction & Fiction Paired Texts* helps emergent readers learn to make connections with both fiction and nonfiction texts. The activities in this book also help fluent readers to enhance and increase their already developing reading skills. *Nonfiction & Fiction Paired Texts* is the perfect reading tool for all levels of readers.

The high-interest texts in *Nonfiction & Fiction Paired Texts* contain both fiction and nonfiction passages. The units are written in pairs that share a common idea or theme. The first passage in each unit is fiction. A nonfiction text follows each fiction story. Subjects in each unit are varied, providing a multitude of topics to engage the various interests of the readers. Topics are also age-appropriate and will appeal to children in the corresponding grade level. While reading the texts, students are encouraged to look for specific meanings and to make logical inferences from what is read.

Each unit in *Nonfiction & Fiction Paired Texts* has five pages. The texts in each set are followed by two assessment pages that contain multiple-choice questions and short-answer writing activities. These pages are designed to meet the rigor demanded by the Common Core State Standards. Each assessment leads students to look for and generally cite textual evidence when answering questions. A third page in the assessment section of each unit includes longer writing activities. The writing activities for each unit are tied to higher-order thinking and questioning skills. The writing ideas are designed to help assess a student's ability to respond to a written prompt while incorporating the skills of excellent writing.

Nonfiction & Fiction Paired Texts was written to help students gain important reading skills and practice responding to questions based on the Common Core State Standards. The different units provide practice with a multitude of standards and skills, including but not limited to the following:

- making and understanding connections between content-rich reading materials

- building reading-comprehension skills

- analyzing, comparing, and contrasting fiction and nonfiction texts

- sequencing and summarizing

- experience with text-based, multiple-choice questions

- practice with short-answer responses

- practice in developing written responses to various prompts

- understanding the genres of fiction and nonfiction texts

- quoting from texts to complete assessments

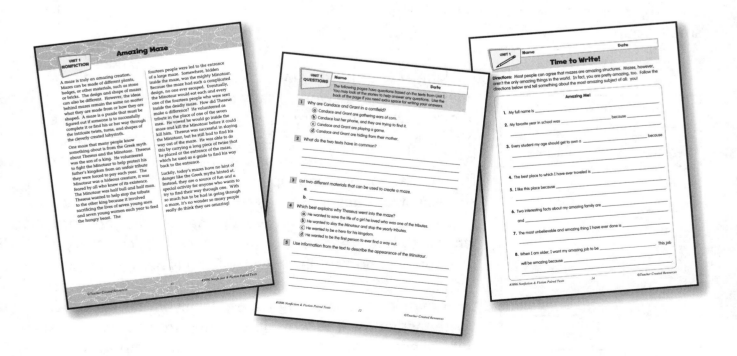

How to Use This Book

Nonfiction & Fiction Paired Texts is divided into twenty-six units. Each unit has five pages. The first two pages are texts that share a common topic or theme. Each unit contains both a fiction and nonfiction selection, as well as three assessment pages.

The book is designed so that each unit can be used separately. The activities can be completed in order, starting with the first unit and working through unit twenty-six, or they can be completed in random order. Anyone using the book may want to look for common themes or ideas that correspond with other units being taught in other subject areas. The units in this book can be used to help teach across the curriculum and to easily tie in reading and writing skills to other areas of study.

Provided with each set of fiction and nonfiction stories are three pages of assessment activities. Two of the three pages are multiple-choice and short-answer questions, which rely heavily on text-based answers. The last page in each unit is a writing page. The teacher may choose to use all three pages after completion of the connected texts, or he or she may choose to only use specific pages for assessment. Pages can be done during regular academic hours or be sent home for extra practice. Students may work on assignments alone or work with partners or in small groups.

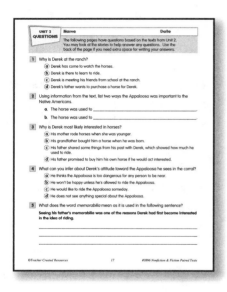

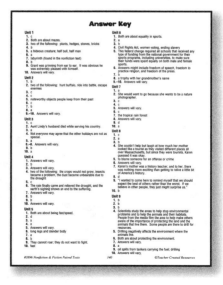

Looking at the answer key, one will notice that not all questions have answers. Many questions require short answers, which can vary, as long as the answers are based on the text. The Common Core State Standards require students to support their answer choices with information from texts, not personal opinions. Completion of the short-answer questions gives students the opportunity to practice writing their answers using information from what they have read in each unit. Of course, creativity is an equally important learning tool and is not ignored in these units. Students are given opportunities to express their own ideas and thoughts, especially in the Time to Write! activities. The writing activities are tied to the texts but are geared to give students the chance to practice the skills needed to be successful writers.

In grading the short-answer questions, teachers must verify that the answers are included in the text. Assessing the responses in the Time to Write! section is up to the teacher's discretion. Each teacher knows the abilities of the individual students in his or her class. Answers provided at one point in the year may be considered satisfactory; however, as the year progresses, the teacher's expectations of the student's writing skills will have greatly increased. A student would eventually be expected to provide better-developed responses and written work with fewer mistakes. A good idea is to keep a folder with samples of the student's work from different times during the academic year. Teachers, parents, and students can easily see progress made with the skills necessary for good writing by comparing samples from earlier in the year to the student's present writing samples.

The units in *Nonfiction & Fiction Paired Texts* can also be used to help students understand the basic principles of text. One way to do this is to teach students to use a specific reading method. Students can use the UNC method (see pages 8–9) to help gain a better understanding of how text is presented on the page and to develop and refine skills for reading for detail. After the UNC method is mastered, students will learn to automatically employ these skills in their everyday reading without having to be coached to complete the process. The skills of good reading will become automatic.

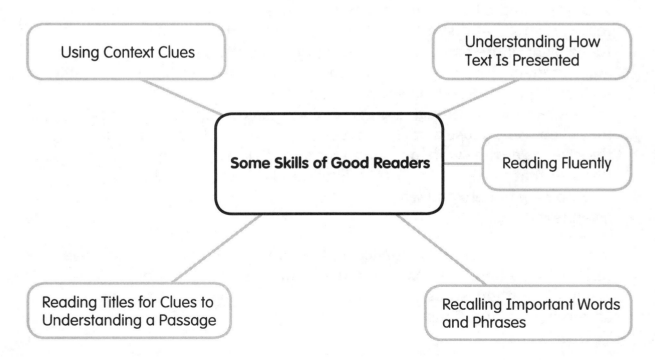

Using Context Clues

Understanding How Text Is Presented

Some Skills of Good Readers

Reading Fluently

Reading Titles for Clues to Understanding a Passage

Recalling Important Words and Phrases

Understanding and Using the UNC Method

U <u>Underline</u> and read all titles.

N Place <u>numbers</u> by all the paragraphs.

C Put <u>circles</u> around or highlight all important words and phrases in the text.

When students are presented with a text, they can use the UNC method to help break down the material. Students immediately underline and read all titles. To better manage the material, students next add a number beside each paragraph. This helps teachers as they go over questions. They can easily ask the students to look at a specific paragraph to point out information that helped to answer a particular question. Using this method, teachers may also discover there are students who have simply not learned how to tell where a paragraph begins or ends. This explains why many times when a teacher asks a student to read a specific paragraph, he or she cannot. The student may honestly be unsure of where to start!

The final step in the UNC method is to circle or highlight important words or phrases in the text. By completing this step, students are required to read for detail. At first, the teacher may find that many students will want to highlight entire paragraphs. Teachers will want to use a sample unit to guide students through the third step. Teachers can make copies of a unit already highlighted to help show students how to complete the third step. Teachers can work through a unit together with the students, or they may even want to use a document camera so the students can easily see the process as they work on a unit together in class. Students will soon discover that there are important details and context clues that can be used to help understand which information is the most important in any given text.

Students need to have confidence in their abilities to succeed at any given task. This is where the UNC method is a bonus in any classroom. When using this method, students can be successful in reading any text and answering the questions that follow.

The UNC method is especially helpful in aiding students to carefully read new or unfamiliar texts. Highlighters are helpful when working with printed texts but are not necessary. (For example, students can use different highlighter colors to complete each step.) Students who consistently use this method will eventually no longer need to physically highlight or circle the text as the necessary skills to great reading become an automatic response with any text. Students who consistently practice the UNC method make mental maps of what they have read and often no longer need to look back at the text when answering the questions! The UNC method allows students who are kinesthetic learners to have a physical activity that can take place during a reading activity. Visual learners are greatly aided by this method, as well. Students are encouraged by their positive progress and look forward to the challenge of reading a new text.

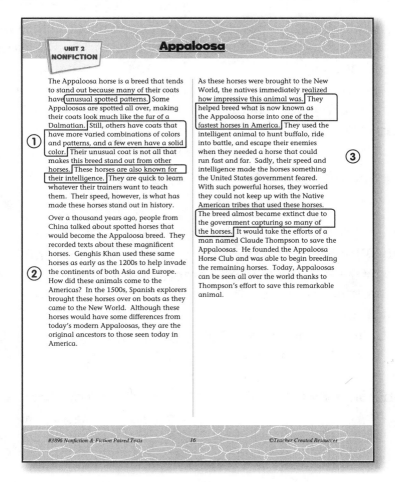

Candace hid among the cornstalks. She was waiting to see if her brother would find her. The game of hide-and-seek was more fun than ever when they played inside the corn maze. Two years ago, Candace's family started growing a field of corn to be made into a maze. The maze added a new attraction to the farm. Her family lived on a sixty-acre farm. They offered tours of their farm each fall. People came to see many things while visiting, such as the pumpkin patch, animals, and corn maze. When visitors were not at the farm, the maze became a playground for Candace and her brother.

"Found you!"

"Grant," Candace said as she twirled around and faced her brother, "how did you sneak up on me? I can usually hear you coming a mile away."

Grant was grinning from ear to ear. He rarely beat Candace in a game of hide-and-seek. It was obvious he was extremely pleased with himself.

"I almost didn't find you, but I saw part of your pink jacket when I was a few rows over. I stayed low and tried to stay on the path. That way, I didn't make as much noise by running into all the cornstalks. I also got lucky when the helicopters flew over the field. They made enough noise that you didn't even notice I was sneaking up behind you."

Candace hated to admit that Grant had won the game, but she did, reluctantly. Just then, both Candace and Grant heard their mother hollering for them. They knew the sound of her voice meant dinner was on the table. The only problem was, Candace wasn't sure she remembered which way to go to get out of the maze.

"I'll admit you beat me this time," Candace finally said to her brother, "but if you really want to show me how clever you are, lead us out of this maze and home for supper."

Grant gave one short nod before taking off with Candace close on his heels. She sighed, knowing she would have to beat him to the kitchen table, or he would never let her live this down.

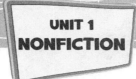

Amazing Maze

A maze is truly an amazing creation. Mazes can be made of different plants, hedges, or other materials, such as stone or bricks. The design and shape of mazes can also be different. However, the ideas behind mazes remain the same no matter what they are made from or how they are shaped. A maze is a puzzle that must be figured out if someone is to successfully complete it or find his or her way through the intricate twists, turns, and shapes of the cleverly created labyrinth.

One maze that many people know something about is from the Greek myth about Theseus and the Minotaur. Theseus was the son of a king. He volunteered to fight the Minotaur to help protect his father's kingdom from an unfair tribute they were forced to pay each year. The Minotaur was a hideous creature; it was feared by all who knew of its existence. The Minotaur was half bull and half man. Theseus wanted to help stop the tribute to the other king because it involved sacrificing the lives of seven young men and seven young women each year to feed the hungry beast. The fourteen people were led to the entrance of a large maze. Somewhere, hidden inside the maze, was the mighty Minotaur.

Because the maze had such a complicated design, no one ever escaped. Eventually, the Minotaur would eat each and every one of the fourteen people who were sent inside the deadly maze. How did Theseus make a difference? He volunteered as tribute in the place of one of the seven men. He vowed he would go inside the maze and kill the Minotaur before it could kill him. Theseus was successful in slaying the Minotaur, but he still had to find his way out of the maze. He was able to do this by carrying a long piece of twine that he placed at the entrance of the maze, which he used as a guide to find his way back to the entrance.

Luckily, today's mazes have no hint of danger like the perils mentioned in the Greek myths. Instead, they are a source of fun and a special activity for anyone who wants to try to find their way through one. With so much fun to be had in going through a maze, it's no wonder so many people really do think they are amazing!

UNIT 1 NONFICTION

The following pages have questions based on the texts from Unit 1. You may look at the stories to help answer any questions. Use the back of the page if you need extra space for writing your answers.

1 Why are Candace and Grant in a cornfield?

    (a) Candace and Grant are gathering ears of corn.

    (b) Candace lost her phone, and they are trying to find it.

    (c) Candace and Grant are playing a game.

    (d) Candace and Grant are hiding from their mother.

2 What do the two texts have in common?

_____

_____

_____

_____

3 List two different materials that can be used to create a maze.

    a. _____

    b. _____

4 Which best explains why Theseus went into the maze?

    (a) He wanted to save the life of a girl he loved who was one of the tributes.

    (b) He wanted to slay the Minotaur and stop the yearly tributes.

    (c) He wanted to be a hero for his kingdom.

    (d) He wanted to be the first person to ever find a way out.

5 Use information from the text to describe the appearance of the Minotaur.

_____

_____

_____

_____

_____

6 Which statement is not a fact?

    (a) Mazes only exist in myths like the text about Theseus and the Minotaur.

    (b) A Minotaur is a mythical creature that is half man and half bull.

    (c) Mazes can be constructed from a variety of materials.

    (d) In the myth, Theseus volunteers to enter the maze.

7 Using information from the texts, write a synonym for the word *maze*.

_____

8 How does Grant feel about winning the game against his sister, Candace?

    (a) He feels extremely upset.

    (b) He feels very happy and excited.

    (c) He feels no extreme excitement.

    (d) He feels confused and worried.

9 Write the sentence(s) from the text that helped you to answer #8.

_____

_____

_____

_____

10 In the Greek myth, Theseus goes into the maze to kill the Minotaur. Think of another solution that could have saved the fourteen tributes. Write your idea on the lines.

_____

_____

_____

_____

_____

_____

Time to Write!

Directions: Most people can agree that mazes are amazing structures. Mazes, however, aren't the only amazing things in the world. In fact, you are pretty amazing, too. Follow the directions below and tell something about the most amazing subject of all: you!

Amazing Me!

1. My full name is _____.

2. My favorite year in school was _____ because _____
   _____.

3. Every student my age should get to own a _____ because
   _____
   _____.

4. The best place I have ever visited is _____.

5. I like this place because _____
   _____.

6. Two interesting facts about my amazing family are _____
   and _____.

7. The most unbelievable and amazing thing I have ever done is _____
   _____.

8. When I am older, I want my amazing job to be _____. This job
   will be amazing because _____
   _____.

The horses pranced around the corral as Derek stood near the fence watching. His father had brought him to the ranch to take riding lessons. Derek had always wanted to learn to ride, but he had never had the chance to try. No one they knew owned any horses, and their house was in the city; having a horse there had never been an option. It wasn't until a few weeks ago that Derek finally knew he was going to have the chance to take a riding lesson. His father had heard about a place only thirty minutes from their home that offered lessons each afternoon. Derek's father would bring him to the ranch after school two days each week. His father already knew how to ride. He had grown up on a farm and had even had his own horse. When he was the same age as Derek and in the sixth grade, he had even started riding horses at shows. He still had some of the ribbons he'd won and several of his trophies. Seeing his father's memorabilia was one of the reasons Derek had first become interested in the idea of riding.

As Derek stared at the different horses, he wondered which horse he would be able to ride. He stared at one horse that seemed faster than all the others. The horse reminded him of a Dalmatian. The horses in the corral were white with black spots. He had read about the Appaloosa horses in a book at the library. The spotted horses were amazingly fast. This was the first time he'd seen one up close. He could understand now why Native Americans loved the unique breed. Even though he loved watching the horse move so quickly, he knew it would be quite some time before he could ride like the wind on such an amazing animal.

"What do you think, Derek?" His father asked, coming up to stand beside him at the fence. "Have you picked out one you want to ride?"

Derek stared longingly at the prancing Appaloosa horse, but then shook his head. "Someday, I hope to be able to ride all of them well, but for right now, I might need to start with the smallest, slowest one they've got. However, I'll pretend I'm riding *that* one," he said, nodding at the fastest horse in the corral.

Appaloosa

The Appaloosa horse is a breed that tends to stand out because many of their coats have unusual spotted patterns. Some Appaloosas are spotted all over, making their coats look much like the fur of a Dalmatian. Still, others have coats that have more varied combinations of colors and patterns, and a few even have a solid color. Their unusual coat is not all that makes this breed stand out from other horses. These horses are also known for their intelligence. They are quick to learn whatever their trainers want to teach them. Their speed, however, is what has made these horses stand out in history.

Over a thousand years ago, people from China talked about spotted horses that would become the Appaloosa breed. They recorded texts about these magnificent horses. Genghis Khan used these same horses as early as the 1200s to help invade the continents of both Asia and Europe. How did these animals come to the Americas? In the 1500s, Spanish explorers brought these horses over on boats as they came to the New World. Although these horses would have some differences from today's modern Appaloosas, they are the original ancestors to those seen today in America.

As these horses were brought to the New World, the natives immediately realized how impressive this animal was. They helped breed what is now known as the Appaloosa horse into one of the fastest horses in America. They used the intelligent animal to hunt buffalo, ride into battle, and escape their enemies when they needed a horse that could run fast and far. Sadly, their speed and intelligence made the horses something the United States government feared. With such powerful horses, they worried they could not keep up with the Native American tribes that used these horses. The breed almost became extinct due to the government capturing so many of the horses. It would take the efforts of a man named Claude Thompson to save the Appaloosas. He founded the Appaloosa Horse Club and was able to begin breeding the remaining horses. Today, Appaloosas can be seen all over the world thanks to Thompson's effort to save this remarkable animal.

UNIT 2 QUESTIONS

Name _____ **Date** _____

The following pages have questions based on the texts from Unit 2. You may look at the stories to help answer any questions. Use the back of the page if you need extra space for writing your answers.

1 Why is Derek at the ranch?

   (a) Derek has come to watch the horses.

   (b) Derek is there to learn how to ride.

   (c) Derek is meeting his friends from school at the ranch.

   (d) Derek's father wants to purchase a horse for Derek.

2 Using information from the text, list two ways the Appaloosa was important to the Native Americans.

   a. The horse was used to _____.

   b. The horse was used to _____.

3 Why is Derek most likely interested in horses?

   (a) His mother rode horses when she was younger.

   (b) His grandfather bought him a horse when he was born.

   (c) His father shared his passion for riding with Derek.

   (d) His father promised to buy him his own horse if he would act interested.

4 What can you infer about Derek's attitude toward the Appaloosa he sees in the corral?

   (a) He thinks the Appaloosa is too dangerous for any person to be near.

   (b) He won't be happy unless he's allowed to ride the Appaloosa.

   (c) He would like to ride the Appaloosa someday.

   (d) He does not see anything special about the Appaloosa.

5 What does the word *memorabilia* mean as it is used in the following sentence?

Seeing his father's memorabilia was one of the reasons Derek had first become interested in the idea of riding.

_____

_____

_____

6 Based on the text, which sentence is not a fact?

(a) The Appaloosa breed is known for its intelligence.

(b) Spanish explorers brought horses to the Americas that were the ancestors of the modern-day Appaloosa.

(c) Everyone knows the Appaloosa is the best breed of horse there is.

(d) The Appaloosa breed almost became extinct.

7 Why does Derek's father most likely support Derek's wish to learn how to ride?

(a) He believes Derek will realize riding is not for him after he tries it.

(b) He enjoyed riding when he was younger, and he wants Derek to have the same experience.

(c) He does not actually support Derek, and he hopes he will not want to continue his lessons.

(d) He is bringing Derek to ride because his wife suggested he spend time with Derek.

8 Why does Derek say he should be given the smallest and slowest horse to ride?

(a) He knows he is an inexperienced rider.

(b) He has always liked slow horses.

(c) He believes all the other horses are already taken.

(d) He is afraid of the other horses.

9 Give an example from the text that shows Derek and his father have a close relationship.

_____

_____

_____

10 What would be a good alternative title for the text "Appaloosa"? Explain your new title choice.

_____

_____

_____

Time to Write!

Directions: Claude Thompson is credited with helping save the Appaloosa horse from extinction. Imagine an animal you love is facing extinction. Use the space below to write a letter to your school or community asking for help in saving your animal. Be sure to list reasons why this animal deserves to be saved.

Remembering

The smell of hamburgers on the grill made Abbie's stomach growl. "The first burgers of the summer" are what her father had called them. Abbie knew he was right; it was the first time they'd pulled out the grill since the weather had warmed up. She knew her father was happy to have a special three-day weekend, too, which would explain why he was smiling and whistling while he cooked their dinner. Abbie wasn't sure what was so special about a longer weekend since she and her brother Jake didn't have to go back to school. Abbie knew the Memorial Day weekend meant a lot of things to a lot of people, but for her, it meant the start of summer break.

Abbie was about to go help her father with the hamburgers when her mother called for her. Abbie opened the screen door on the back porch so she could slide inside. Her mother was busy getting everything ready to make homemade ice cream. Abbie's mouth watered as she thought about the delicious treat. They only had it twice a year. Her mother would make a batch on Memorial Day and then again on Labor Day. Abbie wished she would make it more, but then she knew it wouldn't be as special.

"What's up, Mom?" Abbie asked as she sat down on a nearby chair.

"Your Aunt Lindy called. She wants to know if you can go with her to the cemetery for a few minutes now instead of later today."

Abbie nodded her head. They had all planned to go with her aunt later today, but she didn't mind going now. Abbie watched as her mother sent her aunt a quick text confirming that Abbie would go with her while she finished preparing the meal. Abbie gave her mom a hug and then went outside to the flower garden. She picked a bouquet of flowers for her aunt to place in a vase at the gravesite. Then she waited for her aunt to arrive. She knew Memorial Day was important to Lindy. Her aunt's husband had died while he was deployed to another country. For her aunt, Abbie knew this day was about remembering. Abbie was too young to remember her uncle, but she had heard stories about his heroism and his love for his country. From her family, Abbie had learned that on Memorial Day, people everywhere should remember the sacrifices that had been made for their country.

Memorial Day

There are many different holidays celebrated each year in America, but none are quite as special as Memorial Day. Memorial Day is observed on the last Monday of May. Originally, the holiday honored those who died serving in the military. Today, people continue this tradition; however, many use the day as a time to remember all of those special to them who have passed away.

Memorial Day was first known as Decoration Day. The origins of the holiday began in the years after the Civil War. People wanted a way to honor those who had died while fighting. On the first Decoration Day, nearly 5,000 people helped decorate the graves of the soldiers buried at Arlington National Cemetery. They honored both the Union and Confederate soldiers buried there. Eventually, Decoration Day would become known as Memorial Day. This day would later become a federal holiday recognized by the entire country.

Americans celebrate Memorial Day in different ways. For some, the holiday is seen as the start of the summer season. Others attend special ceremonies or parades in which veterans are recognized for their service to the country. Still, others visit cemeteries and continue with the traditions that Decoration Day once promoted. Some Americans spend each Memorial Day at Arlington National Cemetery. The president of the United States gives a speech there each year. It is at Arlington that the president will place a wreath on the Tomb of the Unknown Soldier to honor all those who have served. The tomb holds the remains of several unidentified soldiers from multiple wars. Even when it is no longer Memorial Day, a soldier remains as a guard at the tomb.

In recent years, one more addition has been made to Memorial Day. At 3:00 p.m. on Memorial Day, each person is asked to take a moment and be still and silent. He or she is to think about and remember all those who have died so that America and its citizens can be free.

UNIT 3
QUESTIONS

Name _____ **Date** _____

The following pages have questions based on the texts from Unit 3. You may look at the stories to help answer any questions. Use the back of the page if you need extra space for writing your answers.

1 Why are Abbie and her family having a cookout?

(a) It is Labor Day weekend.

(b) It is Abbie's birthday.

(c) It is Memorial Day weekend.

(d) It is a homecoming party for Abbie's aunt.

2 Explain why Memorial Day has a special meaning for Abbie's family.

_____

_____

_____

3 Which statement from the text is an opinion?

(a) There are many different holidays celebrated each year in America, but none are quite as special as Memorial Day.

(b) Memorial Day was first known as Decoration Day.

(c) Americans celebrate Memorial Day in different ways.

(d) At 3:00 p.m. on Memorial Day, each person is asked to take a moment and be still and silent.

4 Explain why the answer you chose for #3 is an opinion and not a fact.

_____

_____

_____

5 Which statement best explains why Memorial Day was once known as Decoration Day?

(a) People would clean up and decorate the cemeteries where the soldiers were buried.

(b) People bought decorations for their summer cookouts.

(c) Young girls placed decorations in their hair to honor the deceased soldiers.

(d) No one knows why Memorial Day was once called Decoration Day.

6 Explain why the text is titled "Remembering."

_____

_____

_____

7 Compare and contrast Memorial Day to one other holiday you know. List one way they are alike, and list one way they are different.

Holiday: _____

a. They are alike because _____

_____.

b. They are different because _____

_____.

8 Explain why the Tomb of the Unknown Soldier is an important symbol.

_____

_____

_____

_____

9 What does the word *origins* mean as it is used in the following sentence?

The origins of the holiday began in the years after the Civil War.

  (**a**) ending

  (**b**) beginning

  (**c**) middle

  (**d**) after

10 What is significant about Memorial Day weekend to Abbie?

  (**a**) It is the start of summer vacation.

  (**b**) It is the start of a new school year.

  (**c**) It is a three-day weekend.

  (**d**) It is her favorite holiday.

Time to Write!

Part 1

Directions: Choose one holiday from the list of holidays below or think of one on your own. Circle your choice or write it on the line provided. With the help of your teacher, use books or the Internet to research facts about the holiday. On the lines below, write five facts you learn from your research.

Christmas	**Kwanzaa**	**Thanksgiving**
Hanukkah	**Labor Day**	**Valentine's Day**
Independence Day	**Native-American Day**	**Veterans Day**

Other: _____

1. _____

2. _____

3. _____

4. _____

5. _____

Part 2

Directions: Imagine the holiday you researched is about to be taken off the calendar and no longer celebrated! Write a letter to the president, explaining why the holiday is important and should remain an important day for everyone to celebrate.

Dear President _____,

_____

_____

_____

_____

_____

Sincerely,

_____

Finn stood beside his grandfather, staring out at the crops that were dying in the field. His grandfather had planted acres of corn that were in desperate need of water. If the rain didn't come soon, Finn knew the crop could not survive a continued drought. He wished he knew a way to help, but he couldn't make it rain and neither could his grandfather. The sound of thunder rumbling in the distance brought the only hope they had been given in weeks.

"The clouds are moving fast." His grandfather's voice seemed to rumble deep in his chest, much like the noises of thunder overhead. Finn knew it was probably his imagination, but he almost felt like his grandfather was such a powerful man that he could simply will the rain to come, and it would have to come.

"Does that mean it will rain?" Finn asked.

His grandfather nodded his head slowly, and a small grin tugged at the corners of his mouth. "I think it just might, Finn. I can smell the rain in the air. It's close. It's definitely close."

Finn tilted his face to the clouds. He breathed in deeply. He wanted to smell the rain the way his grandfather had. He wanted to know the rain was close. He wanted to believe that the crop would be saved and that the earth would have all the water it needed. Thoughts raced through his head as the first drop of rain fell on to his cheek. He looked at the black clouds overhead and glanced quickly toward his grandfather. He watched as the first drop hit against his arm. He saw the relief in his grandfather's eyes as more and more drops fell from the clouds. Finn thought he could hear the earth sigh.

"Are we going inside, Grandfather?"

"Not today," he answered. "Let's find a seat on the porch and listen to the sound of the rain on the roof. Today, I believe it just might sound like music to my ears."

Finn listened. He could hear the music. The sound was perfect.

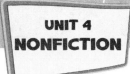
Dust and Drought

From 1931 to 1937, the central regions of the United States, including such states as Oklahoma, Texas, Kansas, and Nebraska, were negatively affected by severe droughts. The area affected spread all the way from Texas to Canada. This lack of rain made life nearly unbearable for those who tried to live there during these years. One area where the drought was the most severe simply became known as the Dust Bowl.

People in this area were farmers. The lack of rain made it nearly impossible to grow any type of crop. What little rain they did receive was never enough.

Grasshoppers were another enemy of the struggling farmers. Anything that did grow was immediately consumed by the insects. Grasshoppers were even known to consume the clothes people hung out on lines to dry. If there were no crops to eat, they would find food in the natural fibers that made up the farmers' clothes.

The soil became so dusty that winds blowing across the prairie would churn the dust into huge clouds that would cover entire towns. The storms formed walls of dust that made it hard for people to breathe. Much of the dust found its way into the lungs of the men, women, and children who lived on the plains.

Because water was scarce, people had to be careful with how much they used. People needed water to drink and to wash their clothes. The storms caused the dust to seep into the cracks of houses. It would cover everything inside a home; however, there wasn't enough water to make everything clean again.

Eventually, new farming methods helped minimize the impact of the storms that brought so much dust to the area. Today, modern farmers know to protect the soil. They even plow in special ways to stop the soil from blowing when the winds move across the prairies. No one can control the rain, but through better methods of farming, the devastation that occurred in the 1930s should never happen again.

The following pages have questions based on the texts from Unit 4. You may look at the stories to help answer any questions. Use the back of the page if you need extra space for writing your answers.

1 Explain why the text is titled "Looking for Rain."

_____

_____

_____

2 Which choice best defines the word *drought*?

   a an unusually large amount of rain

   b a continuous lack of rain

   c a lack of rain combined with continuous wind

   d a series of severe thunderstorms

3 Write the sentence(s) from either text that best helped you to answer #2.

_____

_____

_____

4 Give two reasons why the 1930s weather was so hard on those who lived in the area known as the plains.

   a. _____

_____

   b. _____

_____

5 Why are Finn and his grandfather outside near the fields?

   a They are checking to see if the crop is ready to harvest.

   b They are looking for something Finn left outside.

   c They are checking the condition of the crop.

   d They are looking for a place to dig a well.

6 Explain the meaning of the expression that is boldfaced in this sentence: Finn thought he could **hear the earth sigh**.

_____

_____

_____

_____

7 A simile makes a comparison using the words *like* or *as*. Complete the following similes.

   a. The land was as dry as a _____.

   b. The drought was like a _____.

8 According to the text, why were grasshoppers a problem for farmers?

   (a) They drank all the water.

   (b) They ate any crop that tried to grow and also ate fibers from cloth.

   (c) They were a good food source, but they were too small to make a substantial meal.

   (d) They attacked the livestock.

9 Finn's grandfather's voice is compared to

   (a) the whistle of a train.

   (b) the rumble of thunder.

   (c) the clap of lightning.

   (d) the sound of silence.

10 Explain how you know Finn and his grandfather have a close relationship.

_____

_____

_____

_____

_____

Time to Write!

Directions: In the text "Looking for Rain," compare and contrast conditions during the drought with conditions after the rain came. Use the divided space below to draw two pictures representing the two different conditions. Then use words to describe each illustration. Write the descriptions on the lines below each picture.

During the Drought	**After the Rain**

_____   _____

_____   _____

_____   _____

_____   _____

_____   _____

On Your Mark

On your mark. Get set. Go! Cassidy pushed off quickly from the side of the pool with the tips of her toes. She wanted to have every advantage she could against the girls who were swimming beside her. Today's race would mean the difference between a first-place medal and a second-place medal for her school. She was determined she would not let the swim team down. Her arms stretched out as she made each stroke. The muscles in her legs helped push her forward through the water and down the lane that was marked off just for her. With only one more lap to go, she felt like she was doing well. She knew the girl beside her had won first place last year. She would be Cassidy's toughest competitor to beat, but somehow, she knew she could win. She felt like the race belonged to her.

She touched the wall and lifted her head from the water to wait for the final results. As the announcement came that she had won, she was grateful but not surprised. She knew she had done her best. She had wanted a first-place win, and she had gotten it.

After the race, the girls who had competed all congratulated each other on a good race. Cassidy got out of the pool and was about to go to the locker room to change when she heard the speaker come on for a special announcement.

"Ladies and gentlemen," the voice said. "May I have your attention, please? As you all are aware, Dover High School's Cassidy Smith won first place during the last event. What you may not be aware of is Miss Smith has just set a new record for this event. She finished the race with a record time of exactly two minutes. She beat the previous time by three seconds. Now that is one fast swimmer! Congratulations to Dover High School and Cassidy Smith."

Cassidy could not believe it. She knew she'd been fast, but she could not believe she now held the record for the best time. If only she could be as fast at cleaning her room. Then life would perfect!

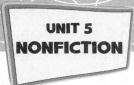
Have you ever tried to do something really fast? Most people have run in a race or have been involved in a sport or competition in which speed was important. Yet, no matter how hard humans try to be fast, some animals in nature will always be faster. One such example is the cheetah. No matter how fast a runner trains to be, he or she will never be a match for the speed of the cheetah.

Cheetahs are stunning-looking cats with long legs and unusual spotted coats. Their long legs and slender bodies aid them in running swiftly. In fact, cheetahs are the fastest animals on the ground and can run at speeds of seventy miles an hour. Their super speed is bad news for their prey. These carnivores eat meat, and their fast legs help them catch whatever they want to eat. Cheetahs are definitely from the cat family, but they differ in several ways from other wild cats, such as lions and tigers. One unique difference about this cat is its inability to roar. Can they purr? You bet! A happy cheetah can make a lot of purring noise!

Another difference between a cheetah and other cats of the wild is its nature. Cheetahs do not want to fight. They would rather use their speed to run away from danger than to stop and fight. This personality trait has made it hard for cheetahs to survive. Other types of predators often take advantage of their more timid natures by stealing their food and even their young.

Today, the number of cheetahs in the wild is diminishing. Those that exist in the wild can be found in both Africa and Asia. Some cheetahs can be found in captivity. People continue to work diligently to try to stop cheetahs from becoming extinct. Cheetahs in captivity are found in zoos and other proper habitats across the world. The people who interact with these amazing cats have worked to find ways to save the gentle cat from extinction.

The following pages have questions based on the texts from Unit 5. You may look at the stories to help answer any questions. Use the back of the page if you need extra space for writing your answers.

1 What do the two texts have in common?

_____

_____

_____

_____

2 What surprise announcement was made at the swim meet?

(a) The rest of the events were going to be canceled.

(b) Cassidy was disqualified from the race.

(c) They were going to do the race a second time.

(d) Cassidy had set a new record for the fastest time at her event.

3 Which sentence about the text is an opinion?

(a) Cassidy is the best swimmer to ever represent her school.

(b) Cassidy won the swim competition she participated in that day.

(c) Cassidy had the best time recorded for her particular event.

(d) Cassidy was racing beside the girl who won the event last year.

4 Which word best describes Cassidy?

(a) determined

(b) lazy

(c) caring

(d) joyful

5 Using information from the text, explain why your answer for #4 best describes Cassidy.

_____

_____

_____

6 List two physical characteristics of the cheetah that help with its speed.

a. _____

b. _____

7 Which characteristic of the cheetah has often hurt the animal?

(a) unwillingness to fight

(b) quick speed

(c) unusual coloring

(d) inability to roar

8 What do Cassidy and a cheetah have in common?

(a) They both live in Africa.

(b) They are both fast.

(c) They do not like to compete.

(d) They do not get along well with others.

9 List two things that make cheetahs different than other cats in the wild.

a. _____

b. _____

10 Use what you have learned and complete the following analogy: *Turtles* are to *slow* as *cheetahs* are to _____.

Time to Write!

Directions: Make a list of five things that should be done quickly. Then explain why.

> ### Example
> Eating ice cream—It will melt if you aren't quick enough.

Must Do Quickly	**Reason**

1. _____   _____

                                               _____

                                               _____

2. _____   _____

                                                 _____

                                               _____

3. _____   _____

                                                 _____

                                               _____

4. _____   _____

                                                 _____

                                               _____

5. _____   _____

                                                 _____

                                               _____

Something Extra: On the back of the page, make a list of five things that should be done slowly. Then explain why they should be done slowly.

Making the Team

The buzzer reverberated through the gym. Melanie collapsed on the floor, thankful it was finally the end of practice. She sat down on the floor and grabbed her bottle of water, taking large gulps to help satisfy her thirst. She loved playing basketball, but she was always hot and thirsty at the end of a long practice. She tried to explain to her mother on the car ride home that yes, she was tired, but it was a good feeling. It felt like she'd worked hard and accomplished something important. She knew that with each practice, she was getting better, and so was the team. She felt certain they would have another winning season this year.

Melanie's mother turned the air conditioning up for her daughter and handed her some more water while they were stopped at a red light. When the light turned green, she expertly guided the car down the road as she began to speak. "You know, Melanie, there is one other special thing about your practice."

"What's that, Mom?" Melanie asked.

"You get to *have* practice and to do it in a facility that is equal to that of the boys. Your grandmother wanted to play basketball when she was a young girl, but they did not have a girls' team. Your grandmother says everyone would tell the girls there simply wasn't enough money for both the girls and boys to be able to have teams."

Melanie's mouth dropped open in surprise. "But, that's not fair. Why should the boys get the money and the girls be ignored?"

"Luckily," her mother began, "other people felt the same as you. Congress actually had to step in and make sure that money was spent equally for both boys and girls when schools provided sports opportunities."

"So, did it happen in time for Grandmother to ever get to play?"

Melanie's mother smiled. "The next time you are near the trophy case in the gym, look carefully at the names engraved on them. You might just see a name you recognize!"

Equality for Athletes

The United States of America is a democracy. This type of government entitles its citizens to have certain freedoms and rights. These freedoms and rights are guaranteed for American citizens in the Bill of Rights. The Bill of Rights is exactly what its name implies. It is a written bill or document that guarantees the people who are citizens of the United States that they will have their rights protected by the government. Some of the rights many people are familiar with include freedom of speech, freedom to practice religion, and freedom of the press. Many of these freedoms may be familiar to you.

As the United States has grown and changed, so have some of the rights of its people. One example of this type of change was the ending of slavery. Another was helping women become equal citizens to men by giving them the right to vote. Most of these changes are well-known by American citizens. However, many people do not realize that changes had to be made to the Civil Rights Act to gain equality for both male and female athletes in public schools.

In 1972, the United States Congress passed what is known as Title IX. It took several years before changes would begin, and Title IX was not implemented until 1978. What is Title IX? This federal change required all schools that received any type of funding from the national government for their sports programs, including universities, to make sure their funds were spent equally on both male and female sports. Why was this necessary? Before 1978, many schools did not offer equal opportunities in athletics to their female students. Discrimination against female athletes was evident before the change in 1978. Many females could not find a sport to participate in while in high school or college. Those who could, often saw the funds being spent on the male students, leaving the female athletes with inferior equipment and facilities. Title IX effectively ended discrimination against female athletes and helped ensure equal rights for all sports teams.

The following pages have questions based on the texts from Unit 6. You may look at the stories to help answer any questions. Use the back of the page if you need extra space for writing your answers.

1 What do the two texts have in common?

_____

_____

_____

_____

2 What is important about the Bill of Rights?

   (a) It guarantees American citizens certain freedoms and rights.

   (b) It keeps some rights from American citizens.

   (c) It collects taxes to pay for certain freedoms.

   (d) It was the first American document written only by female citizens.

3 What does the word *reverberated* mean as it is used in the following sentence?

The buzzer reverberated through the gym.

   (a) jumped

   (b) echoed

   (c) lumbered

   (d) sauntered

4 According to the text, what is one right of American citizens that has changed over time?

_____

_____

5 Write the sentence(s) from the text that explain(s) what Title IX is.

_____

_____

_____

_____

6 According to the text, list two rights that are given to American citizens in the Bill of Rights.

a. _____

b. _____

7 Which part of the text "Equality for Athletes" best helped you to answer #6?

(a) the title

(b) paragraph 1

(c) paragraph 2

(d) paragraph 3

8 What will Melanie most likely see when she looks in the trophy case?

_____

_____

9 Why does Melanie's mother most likely tell Melanie the story about her grandmother?

_____

_____

_____

_____

10 Explain why the text is titled "Equality for Athletes."

_____

_____

_____

_____

_____

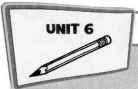

Time to Write!

Part 1

Directions: Title IX was created to help fix a situation that was not fair. What are three things you find unfair? List them below.

1. _____

_____

2. _____

_____

3. _____

_____

Part 2

Directions: Choose one of the topics listed above. Then write a letter to your teacher explaining why the situation is not fair. Provide suggestions to fix this unfair problem.

_____

_____

_____

_____

_____

_____

_____

_____

_____

_____

_____

Maura followed her mother out to the car. She didn't know where they were headed. Her mother had picked her up from school instead of having her ride the bus home, and the only hint she would give Maura was that they were going somewhere special for her birthday. Maura wondered just where they would be going. Normally, Fridays were spent at home eating pizza and watching family movies together, but her mother usually surprised her with something extra special on her birthday. Whatever it was, Maura knew it would be fun.

Maura's mother pulled the car into the parking lot of the mall. As they got out of the car, her mother said, "We are not going to the mall to go shopping. We're going to a new restaurant that's located inside the mall. I know how much you love animals. This restaurant is decorated with all types of animals that live in tropical rain forests. Some are even animated, so it will seem like they are alive, even though they are not."

As they walked into the restaurant, Maura knew she was going to love her birthday surprise. She wanted to be a nature photographer when she grew up. She was always learning all she could about animals and their habitats. She knew right now she could not travel to an actual rain forest, but eating here would feel like the next best thing. As she took her seat at the table, a small frog hopped from one log to another. She knew it wasn't real, but it looked so natural there among all the plants and vines that decorated the restaurant.

If Maura listened closely, she could even hear the sound of rain hitting against the leaves of the tropical plants. She closed her eyes and pretended for a moment that she was in the middle of a real rain forest. She wished she'd brought her camera with her so she could take some pictures. Even if it wasn't real, it felt real.

"I bet I know what you were wishing for," her mother's words broke into Maura's thoughts, and she opened her eyes. In her mother's hand was a brand new camera with a big red bow on top.

Maura had been right; her mother always knew how to make her birthday spectacular.

There are many different types of plants and animals that live in tropical rain forests. Tropical rain forests are areas of thick trees and vegetation that grow in extremely wet regions. Even though these unique habitats are only found in certain parts of the world, they are the homes of more than half of all the plants and animals that exist. Many of these animals are dangerous to man, but in their unusual living conditions, they must be skilled at survival if they are to exist. The rain-forest habitats are full of great beauty but also home to many dangerous predators.

One unique creature that resides in the rain forest is the poison dart frog. These frogs are beautiful to look at with their bright-colored skin. Despite their beauty, they are one of the most dangerous creatures that reside in the forest. They prey on insects, but the poison that comes from the frog's skin can be equally deadly to humans. In fact, some humans use the poison from the frogs on darts, which they use to kill other animals. Just how much poison can one frog produce? The average poison dart frog can make enough poison that it can be deadly to as many as twenty humans!

Army ants are another type of creature that lives in the rain-forest regions. Army ants are small, but their strength comes from their numbers. These ants travel in large numbers to look for their prey. Army ants will attack any size animal to satisfy their hunger for meat. These skillful predators have been known to attack and kill animals that are much larger than they are. Even a ferocious predator like a crocodile is no match for an army of these ants.

Rain forests are filled with many types of plants and animals. This variety adds a beauty to the area that cannot be found in other parts of the world. However, the beauty of the habitat must be looked at carefully. Many of the plants and animals that call the area their home can be deadly to those who do not realize the dangers of this incredible place known as the tropical rain forest.

The following pages have questions based on the texts from Unit 7. You may look at the stories to help answer any questions. Use the back of the page if you need extra space for writing your answers.

1 Why did Maura most likely believe she was going to do something fun on her birthday?

   ⓐ Her mother usually planned fun birthday surprises.

   ⓑ She was turning thirteen, so it was a special birthday.

   ⓒ Her father had told her they were doing something special.

   ⓓ One of her friends knew what her mother had planned and had already told Maura all about her birthday surprise.

2 If Maura had the chance to go visit a tropical rain forest, do you think she would or would not want to go? Use information from the text to support your answer.

_____

_____

_____

3 Why are many of the animals that live in the rain forest dangerous?

   ⓐ They all are herbivores and eat only plants.

   ⓑ They all have sharp claws and teeth.

   ⓒ They all must have a way to protect themselves from other predators.

   ⓓ They all live in trees, so they are hidden by all the leaves.

4 Which paragraph in "Rain-Forest Friends?" gives the most information about army ants?

   ⓐ paragraph 1

   ⓑ paragraph 2

   ⓒ paragraph 3

   ⓓ paragraph 4

5 List one fact from the text about army ants.

_____

_____

_____

6 Why is Maura interested in tropical rain forests?

(a) She loves all types of frogs.

(b) She is not really interested in tropical rain forests.

(c) She wants to be a nature photographer.

(d) She loves the sound of rain.

7 What do the two texts have in common?

_____

_____

_____

8 Explain why the title "Rain-Forest Friends?" most likely has a question mark after the word *friends*.

_____

_____

_____

_____

_____

9 Based on the text, which statement is true?

(a) Poison dart frogs only have enough poison to harm small insects.

(b) Poison dart frogs can be found all over the United States.

(c) Poison dart frogs are unique because they are the only frogs that have teeth.

(d) Poison dart frogs can be deadly to humans.

10 How are army ants able to attack prey that are much bigger than themselves?

(a) They attack in large groups.

(b) They trick other animals into attacking their prey.

(c) They are able to grow larger when it is time to attack.

(d) They can only attack prey that is close to their own size.

Time to Write!

Directions: The creatures mentioned in the text "Rain-Forest Friends?" are not the only animals that reside in the regions of the world known as the tropical rain forests. Choose one of the animals listed below. Discover six facts about the animal you choose. Then, on the back of the page, write a report using the facts you have learned.

Bengal tiger	**green anaconda**	**king cobra**
chimpanzee	**harpy eagles**	**red-bellied piranha**
crocodile	**jaguar**	**whistling spiders**

My animal: _____

Facts

1. _____

   _____

2. _____

   _____

3. _____

   _____

4. _____

   _____

5. _____

   _____

6. _____

   _____

The bus pulled over long enough for several of the passengers to get off. Karen followed her parents and brother down the aisle and off the bus. She watched her mother taking picture after picture as they walked down the sidewalk and headed for their final destination. She couldn't help but laugh at how much her mother looked like a tourist as they visited different places all over Massachusetts, but since they were tourists, Karen guessed it was okay.

Karen knew this trip was especially important to her mother, who had planned this vacation for their family over a year ago. She had wanted to travel up the New England coast and stop to see different historical sites along the way. Just yesterday, they had seen Plymouth Rock, and they had walked the same streets the famous Revolutionary War hero Paul Revere had walked. Karen's mother was a history teacher, and to her, there was nothing more exciting than getting to relive a little bit of America's history.

Today's destination was different than the other tourist stops had been so far. Until today, Karen's mother had chosen all the places for them to visit. Today's choice was all Karen's, and she had asked that the family stop and visit the town of Salem, Massachusetts—the place of the infamous witch trials, which took place during the late 1600s.

"Why are we stopping here?" Karen's brother asked as the family continued walking toward the town.

"This is Salem, Massachusetts. Hundreds of years ago, people who lived in this village were falsely accused of being witches. People began to doubt one another and claim that nearly everyone around them was evil. Sadly, many people were thrown in jail or died. I wanted to come here to remind myself that we should expect the best of others rather than the worst. If we believe in other people, they just might surprise us."

"Does this mean you won't be a witch on Halloween this year?" her brother asked.

"Oh no, I have to be a witch," Karen said, "because I still plan to turn you into a frog!"

Hunting for a Witch

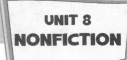

Years ago, people did not understand many things about the world that people now take for granted. One thing that was often a mystery to people was the origin of a disease or sickness. With no modern microscopes to look closely at things that can't be seen by the naked eye, people did not know about germs or the diseases they can cause. When people became sick, our ancestors often looked to supernatural sources as the cause. One such incident happened in the year 1692 in an area that was part of the original thirteen colonies in Salem, Massachusetts.

A young girl by the name of Abigail Williams and her cousin Betty Parris suddenly became sick. The cause of their illness was unknown. The doctor of the small community was perplexed by the girls' condition. Before long, two more girls became sick and seemed to be suffering from the same condition as the previous girls. The doctor proclaimed to everyone in the community that the girls were under the spell of a witch. It was the spell, he proclaimed, that was making them so sick. People were upset by the news, but not shocked, because many people who lived during the late 1600s felt that witchcraft and sorcery were very real, and the practice of these crafts could have serious repercussions for anyone living during this time period.

The girls who had supposedly been bewitched began to accuse others of practicing witchcraft. As more and more people were named as witches, panic began to spread through the town of Salem. In Massachusetts, if a person was accused of practicing witchcraft, he or she could be sentenced to death. Because people were afraid of being accused themselves or of causing accusations to occur against their families, few spoke in defense of those who were accused.

The accused people were brought to trial. Those who confessed to being witches were sentenced to jail. Those who did not were convicted to die. Many people who were innocent confessed to being witches to avoid being put to death. Eventually, the accusations and cries of witchcraft would cease as people began to realize that the evidence simply did not exist to continue to persecute the citizens of Salem. Regardless, such a dark time in America's history should never be forgotten.

The following pages have questions based on the texts from Unit 8.
You may look at the stories to help answer any questions. Use the
back of the page if you need extra space for writing your answers.

1 Why did people who lived long ago look to supernatural sources as the causes of
severe illness?

(a) They thought only witches or ghosts could make people sick.

(b) They had seen so many people get sick, they didn't know what else to think.

(c) They did not yet know about germs and other unseen organisms that could cause an
illness.

(d) They had seen supernatural forces making someone sick.

2 What does the word *repercussions* mean as it is used in the following sentence?

**The practice of these crafts could have serious repercussions for anyone living during this
time period.**

(a) results

(b) promises

(c) endings

(d) beginnings

3 How does Karen feel about her mother taking so many pictures?

(a) She does not like it.

(b) She does not mind it.

(c) She does not understand it.

(d) She ignores it.

4 Write the sentence(s) from the text that helped you to answer #3.

_____

_____

_____

5 What does it mean to accuse someone of something?

_____

_____

6 In today's world, do people blame others for things that did not happen? Explain your answer.

_____

_____

_____

_____

7 Write the sentence(s) that explain(s) why Karen's mother is excited about the family's trip.

_____

_____

_____

8 What can the reader infer about Karen's opinion of others?

(a) She always expects the worst from other people.

(b) She trusts very few people.

(c) She only expects the best from her family.

(d) She believes that there is good in all people.

9 Write the sentence(s) from the text that best helped you to answer #8.

_____

_____

_____

10 Which sentence is an opinion?

(a) A young girl by the name of Abigail Williams and her cousin Betty Parris suddenly became sick.

(b) Such a dark time in America's history should never be forgotten.

(c) Many people who lived during the late 1600s felt that witchcraft and sorcery were very real.

(d) Those who confessed to being witches were sentenced to jail.

Time to Write!

Directions: How would it feel to be falsely accused of something? Imagine another student accused you of cheating or someone said you had taken something that wasn't yours. Tell about a time you (or someone you know) were falsely accused of doing something that is against school rules. Write about the event and how it made you feel. If you need more space, use the back of the page.

Title: _____

_____

_____

_____

_____

_____

_____

_____

_____

_____

_____

_____

_____

_____

_____

_____

_____

_____

_____

Rush to Save

Kyle and Shane were working as fast as they could. They were in a rush to get the donations they had collected to the volunteer organizations that were waiting near the beach. The volunteers were working to help clean up a recent oil spill that had hit the Gulf Coast where both Kyle and Shane's families lived. The two boys were both in sixth grade at Mexico Beach Middle School. The recent oil spill was the first time either boy had experienced a disaster of this type so close to their own homes. Their science teacher, Mr. Jarvis, had been keeping their entire class informed about efforts that were underway to help save the habitats of the affected animals and, of course, the animals themselves. Shane's and Kyle's own parents had encouraged the boys to stay away from the beach while cleanup was underway. Both Kyle and Shane had been shocked at the condition of some of the animals they'd seen in a slideshow Mr. Jarvis had shown the class. Several of the sea turtles in the pictures were so covered in oil that Kyle had whispered to Shane that he doubted they would survive. Mr. Jarvis had heard Kyle's comment and quickly responded with a comment of his own.

"You're right, Kyle. These sea creatures won't survive if we don't step in and help. An oil spill is a huge tragedy. Everyone is affected by it in some way. The animals are innocent victims that need our help."

"How can we help?" Shane had asked.

"We can help best by collecting donations to help the volunteers who are already in place. Many of the organizations that are there to help are trying to clean the oil off the affected animals. They could use special dishwashing detergents to wash the oil off the wounded animals, and they could use more bottled water and extra trained volunteers to aid them with their work."

That afternoon, both Kyle and Shane had stayed after school to talk to Mr. Jarvis. Both had wanted to help. After all, the beach was their home, too, and they felt that they had a responsibility to all the living things that were in distress because of a mistake made by humans. Mr. Jarvis thanked both boys and sent them to gather donations. As the boys hurried to finish their work, they both agreed that what was most important was saving the animals and their natural habitats.

Habitat in Danger

Earth's polar regions are home to many of nature's most magnificent creatures. The frozen lands of the Arctic and Antarctica have some of the harshest living conditions and coldest temperatures on Earth. Despite the frigid temperatures, these lands are home to many animals. Some animals who live in these areas migrate and come back when the temperatures are not as cold. Still others, such as the polar bear and the Arctic fox, stay year-round in the freezing regions they know as home.

Despite the cold, humans have found a way to survive in the polar areas. People have invaded these natural habitats by mining for coal and oil. These invasions by humans have often hurt the wildlife that lives in the area. Because of this, many countries have agreed to stop drilling in these areas to help preserve the habitats of those animals that live there.

Oil spills are also a danger for these regions. Ships that carry oil sometimes sink, and their oil leaks into the ocean. These oil slicks pollute the waters and beaches. The animals living in the water or on the beach can become covered in the oil and can even die if the oil is not removed.

Many people believe that the areas should be protected from pollution. Organizations that protect the wildlife and habitats of the polar regions have made a huge difference in preserving the areas. Scientists have also contributed to saving this natural area by studying the animals that live there and helping find ways to protect them and their habitats. Even the media has played an important role in helping people understand the importance of these animals' habitats by filming television shows and movies, which are shown to those who are unable to visit the regions. People are then able to understand how important these lands are and to see up close the magnificence of those that live there.

UNIT 9 QUESTIONS

Name   **Date**

The following pages have questions based on the texts from Unit 9. You may look at the stories to help answer any questions. Use the back of the page if you need extra space for writing your answers.

1   Why were Kyle and Shane in a hurry to complete their work?

     (a) They had other things they needed to do.

     (b) They needed to get the supplies to the rescue workers.

     (c) The supplies they had were going to expire if they didn't get them delivered.

     (d) They were going to be fired from their jobs if they were late.

2   Based on what you know about Mr. Jarvis, how would he most likely react if another environmental disaster occurred at the beach?

     (a) He would ignore it.

     (b) He would want to volunteer to help.

     (c) He would not care.

     (d) He would try to find a way to make money from the disaster.

3   According to the text, which statement is true about some animals that live in the polar regions?

     (a) The animals with fur have coats that change colors to blend in with their environment.

     (b) Some of the animals leave the Arctic region during certain times of the year and then migrate back to the area.

     (c) The animals only eat food that is found in the ocean.

     (d) Some of the animals cannot migrate because they have no sense of direction and would not be able to return.

4   Based on the text, list one reason why someone might be living in the polar regions.

_____

_____

_____

5   Explain why drilling for oil is harmful to the polar regions.

_____

_____

_____

6 What do the two texts have in common?

_____

_____

_____

_____

7 Mr. Jarvis tells Shane and Kyle that everyone is affected in some way by an oil spill. Explain how Shane and Kyle are affected by the oil spill.

_____

_____

_____

_____

8 Which word best describes Mr. Jarvis?

(a) caring

(b) misinformed

(c) unique

(d) shy

9 According to the text, what is one way that oil sometimes gets into the ocean?

_____

_____

10 What would be a good alternative title for the text "Habitat in Danger"? Explain your new title choice.

_____

_____

_____

_____

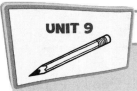

Time to Write!

Directions: Imagine you are planning a carnival to raise money to help save the habitats of the animals that live in the arctic regions. Use the space below to help plan your event. On the back of the page, design a poster for your carnival. Be sure to tell when and where the event will be held.

Why do you believe this event would raise money for your cause?

What type of activities would you have?

Danger at the Lake

Kessler and his sister Katie walked quickly down the worn path toward the lake. After three days of solid rain, the sun was now shining. Neither of them wanted to miss a chance to finally be able to do something outside. A vacation at the lake wasn't much fun if no one in the family could get to the water. It was only a few hours ago that their mother had informed them the rain was moving out and that, by the afternoon, the area around the lake house would be bathed in sunlight. Kessler and Katie had both enjoyed the last few days playing games inside and watching movies with their parents, but with their sixth-grade year starting in just one week, they'd all hoped their last days of summer vacation would be spent outside doing things like fishing and swimming.

As Kessler and Katie reached the end of the path, the sun was shining brightly in the sky. Kessler handed Katie her fishing pole as he grabbed his own pole and their tackle box full of needed supplies. They settled themselves on the dock, ready to enjoy an afternoon of fishing. Their father had told them if they caught enough catfish for the entire family, he would clean them and cook them so they could have a fish fry for supper. As they put their baited hooks into the water, both children could almost taste how delicious the night's meal would be.

It didn't take long from the time Kessler dropped his line into the water for him to yell out, "I've caught a fish!" Katie ran over to see. Kessler began to reel in the line. Whatever was on the other end was fighting to get away. Finally, the hook came up out of the water and Kessler began reeling faster. "That's not a fish!" Katie screamed as Kessler dropped the pole onto the deck. Twisted around Kessler's fishing line was a cottonmouth snake! Amazingly, the snake did not appear to be hooked but was wrapped around the line as though holding on for dear life. The brother and sister moved quickly to the edge of the deck and out of the way of the poisonous snake. They watched as the snake uncoiled itself and slipped back into the water, its head held high, mouth open showing off its cotton white color. As Kessler and Katie ran all the way home, Kessler knew he wanted to fish again, but for now he thought he'd simply tell his parents he was craving pizza for supper.

Cottonmouths: Deadly Danger

There are many different types of snakes, but for those who live in the Southeastern region of the United States, the cottonmouth is one of the most widely known snakes. Cottonmouths are poisonous. Like rattlesnakes, they have a unique feature that often makes them more recognizable than some other types of snakes. The cottonmouth, which is also sometimes known as a water moccasin, has a white or cotton-colored lining on the inside of its mouth. When the snake hunts for food in the water, it lifts its head above the waterline and opens its large mouth. For humans, this habit of the poisonous snake helps make it more recognizable from other snakes that might also live near water.

Cottonmouths live in areas such as rivers, lakes, or swamps. They reside near water because their prey lives in the same areas. Some of their favorite things to hunt include fish, frogs, turtles, and even birds. The coloring on the cottonmouth's scales help the snake to blend in with the land surrounding the water. The mix of black and brown shades on its scales works to camouflage the snake from many of its own enemies that include largemouth bass and great blue herons. Of course, the number one enemy of the cottonmouth snake is humans. Most people have a fear of being bitten by the poisonous snake.

A cottonmouth uses its fangs to insert venom into its victim. The snake also has a powerful, hinged jaw that helps it hang onto its prey, making it nearly impossible for the victim to escape. Once the venom spreads, most small prey die quickly. In humans, the venom also spreads quickly. However, most humans are much larger than the prey generally chosen by cottonmouths. Regardless, the cottonmouth's poison can make a person seriously ill, and in some cases, it may even be deadly for the victim if the person is not treated by a doctor. As the poison enters its victim's body, it attacks the red blood cells and other tissues. The cottonmouth needs its venom to survive, yet it is because of this poison that some people want to see the species eradicated from where they reside.

UNIT 10 QUESTIONS

Name _____ **Date** _____

The following pages have questions based on the texts from Unit 10. You may look at the stories to help answer any questions. Use the back of the page if you need extra space for writing your answers.

1 What unusual feature gives the cottonmouth its name?

(a) The fangs of the snake are snowy white.

(b) The outer edge of the snake's mouth is extremely white.

(c) The mouth of the snake is always extremely dry.

(d) The inside portion of the snake's mouth is white like cotton.

2 What do the two texts have in common?

_____

_____

_____

_____

3 Why do Kessler and Katie stop fishing and return to the lake house?

(a) They decide they are hungry and want to eat some pizza.

(b) They are afraid of being bitten by the snake.

(c) They forgot to bring bait for their hooks.

(d) They remember they don't really like to eat fish.

4 Where would you most likely find a cottonmouth?

(a) in the woods

(b) on the branches of trees

(c) near water

(d) under rocks

5 Write the sentence(s) from the text that best helped you to answer #4.

_____

_____

_____

_____

6 Why are Kessler and Katie anxious to get to the lake?

    (a) They are hungry and need to fish for food.

    (b) They have not been able to get outside because of bad weather.

    (c) They are anxious to go swimming.

    (d) They will have to clean the house if they do not go outside.

7 Explain how the cottonmouth's habit of having its mouth wide open while it swims is beneficial for humans.

_____

_____

_____

_____

8 Based on what you've read, how will Kessler most likely react the next time he goes fishing and feels something in the water tugging at the fishing line?

    (a) He will give the pole to his sister.

    (b) He will check the line carefully.

    (c) He will stop fishing.

    (d) He will throw the pole into the water.

9 Explain why Kessler and Katie's family are at the lake house.

_____

_____

_____

_____

10 Compare the cottonmouth to another animal that is a predator. List two ways the animals are similar.

    Name of animal: _____

    1. _____

    2. _____

Time to Write!

Snake! When you hear the word, what image comes to your mind? Many people are afraid of snakes. Other people love them. Follow the directions below, and write about these incredible reptiles.

Part 1

Directions: Write a persuasive paragraph to convince everyone they should have a snake as a pet. Give at least two reasons why a snake would be an excellent pet.

_____

_____

_____

_____

_____

_____

_____

Part 2

Directions: Write a persuasive paragraph to convince everyone they should not have a snake as a pet. Give at least two reasons why a snake would not be an excellent pet.

_____

_____

_____

_____

_____

_____

_____

A Cheerful Heart

Rachel groaned when she looked at the clock beside her bed. It was time to get up and get moving. Even though it was Saturday morning, Rachel's mother would not let her sleep late today. Her mother had told her just last night that her grandparents were coming to visit for the weekend. Rachel loved seeing her grandparents. She missed them when they were not around, but she did not like getting the house ready for their visits. Her mother thought the house needed to be spotless whenever they came to stay. She and Rachel would spend the day cleaning. Even though Rachel would never admit it to her mother, she liked it when everything was in place and organized. If her mother knew that, she'd have her clean even more than she already did.

Pushing back the covers, Rachel hopped out of bed and walked down the hall to the kitchen. She knew she would need at least a bowl of cereal if she were going to have enough energy to endure the day of deep cleaning. As she got closer to the kitchen, she realized there were many delicious smells coming from the room. Then she saw all of her favorite breakfast foods on the kitchen table. There were pancakes, sausage, bacon, eggs, and biscuits. She noticed, too, that the kitchen was spotless, even though she knew her mother had made all of the delicious foods she saw. Rachel could not believe it. Her mother must have been up for hours cooking and cleaning.

"I can't believe you did all of this," Rachel said, staring at her mother's smiling face.

"I wanted to show you how much I appreciate your helping me today," she explained. "I know you don't like cleaning the house on your day off from school, but you are still willing to help me, and that means a lot to me. I remember when I was young, having to help my mother beat the dust out of all the rugs and polish all of the silver in the house. I would have much rather been playing."

Rachel knew her mother understood. She sat down and took a big bite of her delicious pancakes and vowed to herself that for the rest of the day she would do her best to help without complaining, and she vowed to remind herself to have a cheerful heart whenever she could.

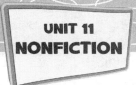
Have you ever thought about how you would keep your house clean without some of the modern conveniences people now have? How would the dirt be cleaned from the floor without the power of a vacuum? How could someone remove all the dust from his or her furniture without a dusting spray and rags? How would things be washed without running water? Years ago, people cleaned their homes in different ways than people do today.

Archeologists study the lives of prehistoric people to better understand the culture and lifestyles of those who lived in the past. As they continue to discover earlier civilizations, one fact they have noticed is that many places had pits that were dug into the earth to help collect garbage. These pits were filled with the things that would have been considered household garbage, such as old bones and broken dishes. Archeologists have also found brushes made from reeds and dried grass that were used to sweep away dust from the floors of homes. Many centuries later, feather dusters would be used to sweep dust from rooms. Unfortunately, the feather dusters did not truly remove any of the dirt from the room; they simply caused the particles of dust to go back onto the place that was just dusted! As a result, dust moved all around a room without ever actually being removed.

Another important part of cleaning that has changed throughout the years is washing and drying laundry. Today, many people have modern washers and dryers. Years ago, gas or electric washers and dryers were not an option. In the late 1800s, an entire day was usually designated as laundry day. By hand, clothes would be washed in large kettles of water and then pounded to remove dirt. Once the clothes were clean, the water was wrung out of them by hand. Damp clothes were either hung outside to dry in the sun or hung in rooms where heat from a fireplace would help finish the process. Ironing was also part of laundry day. Unlike today's modern irons, flatirons could not be plugged into any outlet to operate. The metal irons had to be heated on stoves and then pressed onto the clothes.

Keeping a clean home today is much easier than in the past. Modern conveniences make having a sweet home truly a little sweeter.

The following pages have questions based on the texts from Unit 11. You may look at the stories to help answer any questions. Use the back of the page if you need extra space for writing your answers.

1 How does the reader know Rachel does not want to clean the house?

    a She groans when she first wakes up and thinks about her day.

    b She argues with her mother about having to clean the house.

    c She tells her friends she is upset about her weekend plans.

    d She refuses to talk to her mother.

2 Using information from the text, explain the job of an archaeologist.

_____

_____

_____

3 Explain why the text is titled "A Cheerful Heart."

_____

_____

_____

_____

4 What is one way archeologists know people in prehistoric times tried to keep the areas where they lived clean?

    a They discovered large pits that were used for trash.

    b They discovered pictographs that showed pictures of people cleaning.

    c They discovered gold pots that were used for laundry.

    d They discovered written texts listing the procedures for keeping a dwelling clean.

5 What do the two texts have in common?

_____

_____

_____

_____

6 The next time Rachel's mother asks her to help clean the house, what do you think Rachel's attitude will be? Explain your answer.

_____

_____

_____

7 Why did Rachel's mother cook her breakfast?

    a She wanted to do something nice for her since Rachel was going to help her.

    b She thought Rachel needed to eat more.

    c She only cooks breakfast on Saturdays.

    d She knew Rachel had skipped supper and would be hungry.

8 What does the word _designated_ mean as it is used in the following sentence?

    In the late 1800s, an entire day was usually designated as laundry day.

    a lost

    b assigned

    c ruined

    d missed

9 In your opinion, why is it important to keep the area where you live clean? Give two reasons.

    a. _____

        _____

    b. _____

        _____

10 What would be a good alternative title for the text "Home Sweet Home"? Explain your new title choice.

_____

_____

_____

_____

Time to Write!

Directions: Everyone wants an easier way to clean, including your teacher! Think of something in the classroom that needs to be cleaned each day. Then create an invention or a solution that will make the job easier. Use the space below to define the problem, and then explain how you will solve it.

Problem: _____

Why is this a problem? _____

_____

_____

_____

My invention or solution would be _____

_____

_____

_____.

Someday, if an archeologist discovered our classroom, he or she would probably think

that my invention or solution was (a) _____

because _____

_____

_____

_____

_____.

The Drill

Today, we will practice the procedure for a fire drill," Mr. Faulkner said to his sixth-grade class. "I will need everyone to line up and go out the back door when the signal begins. Once we are outside, I will take attendance to make sure we have everyone safely outside. Are there any questions?"

Perry looked around his classroom to see if anyone else had any questions. When no one spoke, Perry decided to ask the question that was on his mind.

"Mr. Faulkner, has this school ever had a real fire?"

"That's a good question, Perry," Mr. Faulkner said. "We have been very lucky that we've never had any major fires. However, about ten years ago, we did have a small fire in the kitchen. Some oil got on one of the rags, and it resulted in a small fire. Thankfully, everyone was kept safe, and the fire department was able to get the situation under control. That is why it is important for us to practice the drill and know what we need to do. The only mistake we made that day was some of the students lined up in the parking lot right where the fire trucks needed to go, and it caused a small delay in the response time."

"So, where we go when we leave the building is just as important as what we do to get out of the building?" another student asked.

"Absolutely," Mr. Faulkner replied.

Just then, the alarm went off. The drone of the bell reverberated through the classroom. The students rose from their seats and headed out the door in a single-file line. Perry saw the pleased look on Mr. Faulkner's face as everyone performed the drill flawlessly. Perry hoped there would never be a real fire at his school, but he knew if there was, his class would know what to do and would do whatever they were supposed to do without fail. After hearing that there really had been a fire in the school, he didn't doubt that all of his classmates would now realize just how important the fire drills really were.

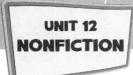

Safety First

Fire can be both a blessing and a curse. Before dealing with anything flammable, people must be willing to learn and understand the appropriate safety measures that should be followed. With good planning and knowledge about fire safety, everyone should be able to enjoy the benefits of a warm fire or even a simple flame without having to worry about things going wrong.

Because a fire can start without much warning, every family should have a plan of action in case of a fire. First, all homes should be equipped with smoke detectors. Fire extinguishers are also good to own, especially in areas where the threat of fire might be greater, such as a kitchen or workshop. For homes with a second story, family members should have a plan for evacuation in case stairs leading down are blocked by fire. All families should have a meeting point outside of the house in case everyone must leave the house. Children often practice fire drills at school, but such drills should also be practiced at home. Children should know that in the event of a fire, they should focus first on getting out of the house safely. No one should ever stop to collect toys or to make phone calls. Everyone in a family should know what the plan is in case a fire happens.

Most people realize that not all fire is bad. There are so many ways that fire is important in the lives of people. Campfires for roasting marshmallows or hot dogs can be a lot of fun. Birthday candles on cakes can bring smiles to everyone. Sometimes controlled fires are even used to help prepare the soil for another year of growing crops.

Fires that quickly get out of control can happen in many different ways. Problems with electrical wires can lead to house fires. People falling asleep while smoking or carelessly throwing clothes on top of a lampshade are both things that can lead to unwanted fires in the home. Combustible items such as paper and wood must be watched carefully while someone is cooking. No matter the occasion, when dealing with any type of flame, people should always think about safety first.

UNIT 12
QUESTIONS

Name

Date

The following pages have questions based on the texts from Unit 12. You may look at the stories to help answer any questions. Use the back of the page if you need extra space for writing your answers.

1 Which is a synonym for the word *procedure* as it is used in the following sentence?

Today, we will practice the procedure for a fire drill.

   a chaos

   b process

   c scenery

   d lesson

2 The text states that fire can be both "a blessing and a curse." Explain this statement.

_____

_____

_____

3 What does the nonfiction text mean when it states that every family should have a plan of action in case there is a fire?

   a They should have a plan for a safe escape.

   b They should have a plan to purchase fire extinguishers.

   c They should have a plan to purchase smoke detectors.

   d They should have a plan for helping their pets to escape from a fire.

4 Why does Mr. Faulkner say it is important for the students to practice the fire drill?

_____

_____

_____

5 Write an opinion statement about fires.

_____

_____

_____

_____

6 Explain why a family would need a meeting place outside of their home if there were a fire inside the house.

_____

_____

_____

7 What can the reader infer Perry will do during the next fire drill?

ⓐ He will laugh and not listen to directions.

ⓑ He will listen and treat the drill as a serious procedure.

ⓒ He will tell anyone who will listen the same thing Mr. Faulkner told him.

ⓓ He will ask to go back inside the building.

8 Explain one way your family might safely use fire.

_____

_____

_____

9 Which word below means the same as the word *evacuation* as it is used in the following sentence?

Family members should have a plan for evacuation in case stairs leading down are blocked by fire.

ⓐ meeting

ⓑ redemption

ⓒ invitation

ⓓ departure

10 What does the title of the text "Safety First" mean in relation to fire safety?

_____

_____

_____

Time to Write!

Directions: Idioms are groups of words that do not mean what the individual definitions of the words usually mean. For example, the idiom "a chip on your shoulder" means someone has a grudge; it does not mean that someone actually has a chip sitting on his or her shoulder.

There are many idioms that contain the word *fire*. Read through the list of idioms below. Then write the meaning of each idiom on the lines. If needed, use the Internet to help you.

Idioms	Meaning
add fuel to the fire	_____ _____
fight fire with fire	_____ _____
several irons in the fire	_____ _____
there's no smoke without fire	_____ _____
fire back	_____ _____
fired up	_____ _____

Something Extra: On the back of the page, draw an illustration to go with the idiom "drawn like a moth to a flame." Be ready to explain the meaning of the idiom.

"Are those nuts in the brownies?" Quinton asked the student who was passing out the food at the party.

She nodded her head yes and Quinton politely declined the chocolate treat. Quinton wasn't even tempted to try the brownie. He could still remember how scary it was last year when he found out he was allergic to nuts. He and his mother had been grocery shopping. The people in the store were handing out free samples of new products. They had both tried several different new foods when, all of a sudden, Quinton felt like his throat was closing up on him. He found it hard to breathe, and he started having severe pains in his stomach. Luckily, his mother understood what was happening. She rushed him to the hospital, and they confirmed that he had a food allergy. Eventually, they were able to identify the culprit in one of the samples they had tried in the store. Quinton had never had an allergic reaction until that day, but now he knew to avoid anything that might cause a reaction. He also kept medicine at his school just in case something like that happened again.

Quinton watched the other children eating their brownies with nuts as he sipped on his juice. Just then, he felt a tap on his shoulder, and he turned around. The same student who had offered him the brownie was standing there. She held out an apple and a banana for Quinton as she said, "I forgot the teacher told us you were allergic to nuts. I had this fruit in my lunchbox, and I thought you might want to have some of this instead."

Quinton smiled at the girl as he took the apple from her and told her thank you. It was not always easy for him to feel different than the other students, but he was glad that she had wanted to include him. With everyone watching out for him, being different was not a bad thing at all!

There are many children who are affected by food allergies. A food allergy can be caused by different types of food. Common causes of allergies include such foods as nuts, seafood, milk, eggs, and wheat. When a person has a food allergy, he or she must make sure to avoid any items that contain the allergen. If the item is accidently ingested or in some cases, even touched, the person may develop a variety of symptoms including but not limited to shortness of breath, wheezing, coughing, nausea, vomiting, and stomach pains. The most serious allergic reactions can cause anaphylaxis. This sudden and severe allergic reaction causes many different symptoms or side effects to happen all at once. Although many children are affected by various food allergies, some will outgrow them. Each case is unique and must be handled in a way that keeps the affected person safe and secure.

If someone is experiencing symptoms of an allergy, it is very important to go to the doctor and find out if an allergy is at fault. A doctor who specializes in allergies is the best to see and ask for help. He or she will ask about any previous events or reactions to food. One test a food allergist might use is a skin test. A skin test consists of placing a small drop of liquid on a small scratch on the patient's skin. The doctor will place a variety of different liquid substances on the small scratch to see how the patient reacts to each one. A raised spot on the skin will reinforce that the person does, indeed, have an allergy. The doctor and his staff will then find out what the patient is allergic to, so the person can then avoid exposure to the substance that causes the allergic reaction.

Once a person is identified as having a specific allergy, a plan will be prepared to help the person manage the condition. One way for the patient to be protected is to be given a list of foods that are considered safe to eat. Anyone who has a food allergy must also have a plan of action in case he or she makes a mistake and accidently ingests something that may cause a reaction. Having a food allergy may not always be fun, but the good news is that with diligence and a clear plan, the condition can definitely be managed.

UNIT 13 QUESTIONS

Name _____ **Date** _____

The following pages have questions based on the texts from Unit 13. You may look at the stories to help answer any questions. Use the back of the page if you need extra space for writing your answers.

1 What do the two texts have in common?

_____

_____

2 Which statement is not true about food allergies?

(a) A person with a food allergy must watch what he or she eats.

(b) A person with a food allergy may outgrow the allergy.

(c) A person with a food allergy can never attend any social functions where that food is served.

(d) A person with a food allergy must have a clear plan to avoid possible complications with food.

3 Which part of the text in "Food Allergies" best explains the symptoms that can happen if someone is allergic to a certain food source?

(a) the title

(b) paragraph 1

(c) paragraph 2

(d) paragraph 3

4 Which word best describes how Quinton handles his food allergy?

(a) diligently

(b) carelessly

(c) spontaneously

(d) recklessly

5 Explain why a doctor would perform a skin test on a patient who has a suspected food allergy.

_____

_____

_____

_____

6 What is an anaphylactic reaction?

(a) a nonthreatening allergic reaction

(b) an extremely serious allergic reaction

(c) an allergic reaction to plants and animals

(d) an allergic reaction to any type of food

7 Write the sentence(s) from the text that helped you to answer #6.

_____

_____

_____

_____

8 Explain why a person would need a plan to help manage a serious food allergy.

_____

_____

_____

_____

9 Which is true about Quinton?

(a) He was born with his food allergy.

(b) He had a food allergy, but he outgrew his food allergy.

(c) He was embarrassed about having a food allergy.

(d) He showed no symptoms of a food allergy when he was a baby.

10 Why does the girl in Quinton's class offer him a piece of fruit?

(a) She wants him to have a snack like the rest of the class.

(b) She knows he only eats fruit.

(c) She does not want her fruit.

(d) She was going to throw the fruit away.

Time to Write!

Directions: Use the space below to create a superhero who fights food allergies. Follow each step to complete your important task.

Step #1: Draw and color a picture of your allergy-fighting superhero.

Step #2: Explain your superhero's powers. How will he or she fight off food allergies? What special powers does he or she have that helps him or her succeed in the fight against the foods that cause the allergies?

_____

_____

_____

_____

_____

_____

_____

It was Halloween night, and Jeremy and Scarlett were getting ready to go trick-or-treating. Their mother stood at the bottom of the stairs becoming increasingly more impatient. "If you two don't hurry up, all the other kids will have gotten all the candy, and you won't get any," she yelled up at them as she tapped her foot. It was already after eight, and she wanted the children back home and in bed by ten.

"Okay, we're almost ready!" Scarlett yelled down at her mother. Then she heard the twins scampering about at the top of the stairs and Jeremy clearing his throat dramatically.

"Now presenting," he yelled, using his best announcer voice, "ancient Egyptian mummies!" Then the two children walked down the stairs trying hard not to trip. What their mother saw made her want to burst into laughter, but she held back her chuckling as she watched the children descend the stairs.

The previous week, she had purchased very nice costumes from the Halloween store for both of them. For Jeremy, she had bought a zombie costume, and for Scarlett, she had purchased a witch costume, but neither of them had wanted to wear the store-bought outfits. Their mother had told them that if they could come up with different costumes, then they were free to wear them, and now here they were.

The twins had taken turns wrapping themselves in toilet paper and tape and had even cut little holes out right where their mouths and eyes were. They marched down the stairs, feeling quite proud of themselves and ready to trick-or-treat. Their mother smiled down at them and handed them their candy buckets.

"Ready to trick-or-treat, little mummies?" she asked.

The two jumped up and down, tripping over some of the toilet paper as they shouted their approval. Their mother shook her head and pushed them out the door, laughing as she noticed that both of her mummies had a trail of toilet paper stuck to their shoes.

Marvelous Mummies

Mummies are preserved bodies of once living things such as people and animals. Some of the most well-known mummies are the mummies of ancient Egypt. The ancient Egyptians are famous for their elaborate burial processes and ceremonies. Just the wrapping of the body could take up to fifteen days of work.

Ancient Egyptians used natural salts to first dry out the body to prepare it for the mummification process and stop it from rotting away. Drying the body usually took forty days, but even before the drying, the internal organs had to be removed due to the fact that they decayed quickly. The only organ that would be left after this intricate process was the heart, which they believed the mummy would need to be judged in the afterlife. To help the mummy keep its shape, the body would be packed with linen, sand, or even sawdust. After the drying procedure, the body was rubbed with oils to keep the skin from cracking. This whole process took up to seventy days. Then, it was time to wrap the mummy.

The Egyptians would use hundreds of yards of linen to carefully wrap the mummy. As many as twenty layers of fabric have been found on one mummy. But even with layer upon layer of cloth, the bandages were kept tight enough to keep the mummy's shape. Amulets and jewelry were occasionally placed in between layers, along with a liquid resin used to harden and glue each layer together.

After the embalming and bandaging processes, the mummy would be placed inside a coffin or special case. The design of the coffins varied throughout Egyptian history. The first mummy cases were plain, wooden boxes, but soon body-shaped cases became popular. Designs and hieroglyphs were painted on the outside, giving each case its own personal look. The ancient Egyptians were adamant about the process and the way their dead were preserved because they strongly believed in a better afterlife. They went through long and drawn out ceremonies to respect and honor their dead.

The following pages have questions based on the texts from Unit 14. You may look at the stories to help answer any questions. Use the back of the page if you need extra space for writing your answers.

1 Why were Scarlett and Jeremy dressed up?

(a) They were dressed up for a costume party.

(b) They were dressed up to go trick-or-treating.

(c) They were dressed up to scare their mother.

(d) They were dressed up to play a game.

2 What is one thing that makes the two texts similar?

_____

_____

_____

_____

3 Which adjective best describes the ancient Egyptians' methods for preserving their dead?

(a) haphazard

(b) chaotic

(c) disorganized

(d) methodical

4 List the two household materials that Jeremy and Scarlett used to make their costumes.

a. _____

b. _____

5 Write the sentence(s) from the text that helped you to answer #4.

_____

_____

_____

_____

6 Why was the heart the only internal organ the ancient Egyptians left inside the mummy?

   (a) They believed that the heart contained the mummy's soul and should not be disturbed.

   (b) They believed that the mummy would need the heart to be judged in the afterlife.

   (c) They believed that the heart protected against evil spirits.

   (d) They believed that the heart was filthy and should never be handled.

7 Which would be a good alternative title for the text "Marvelous Mummies"?

   (a) "The Mummification Process"

   (b) "Mummies Are Gross"

   (c) "Embalming Mummies"

   (d) "Modern Mummies"

8 Which is a synonym for the word *embalming*?

   (a) decomposing

   (b) preserving

   (c) decaying

   (d) putrid

9 What two store-bought costumes did Jeremy and Scarlett's mother get them?

   a. _____

   b. _____

10 Why was the body of the deceased rubbed with oils after the drying process?

   _____

   _____

   _____

Time to Write!

Directions: The ancient Egyptians went through long and extremely detailed processes to preserve the dead. Pretend you're an ancient Egyptian. Would you rather be buried or preserved through these processes? Tell why or why not. Are there some parts of the processes you agree with and others you don't? Write an essay answering the previous questions.

_____

_____

_____

_____

_____

_____

_____

_____

_____

_____

_____

_____

_____

_____

_____

_____

_____

_____

_____

_____

_____

_____

_____

Rock and What?

Luke had his earphones in and the volume up. The music was playing loudly as he closed his eyes and nodded his head to the beat. The only thing that he could hear was the rock music coming though his earbuds. He could not hear his best friend, Cal, trying to talk to him.

"Hey, which video game do you want to play?" Cal asked as he inspected two cases.

When Luke didn't respond, Cal looked up only to realize his friend had his music so loud that he could hear it from the other side of the couch. He leaned over and pulled out one of the earbuds, causing Luke to snap his eyes open and sit up.

"Why'd you do that?" Luke asked. As Luke took off the earbuds, he shook his head from side to side. He noticed that there was a slight ringing sound in his ears.

"I was asking you which video game you wanted to play," Cal explained.

"What?" Luke's eyebrows pulled together at his friend's words. To him, they sounded muffled, like he had cotton in his ears.

"I said, which game?" Cal held up two games for emphasis.

"What?" Luke asked again, this time his voice a little too loud.

"Dude. Video Games. Choose." Cal rolled his eyes.

"I honestly cannot understand a word you're saying," Luke responded. Cal's voice still sounded distorted to his ears.

Cal decided to try to speak louder for Luke's benefit. "I think you might have messed up your hearing. Your music was too loud!" Cal pointed to his own ears and made wild gestures as he talked, trying to make his words understood. This only served to confuse Luke more.

"What did you say?"

Cal groaned and rolled his eyes once more. Luke had messed up his hearing because of listening to his rock and roll music too loud. So much for gaming night.

Hearing Loss from Earbuds

Have you ever heard a loud noise for a long period of time and later felt as if everything you heard was muffled? Loud noises can cause serious damage to your ears and hearing, and believe it or not, so can earbuds. Earbuds are small speakers that you connect to a music player or your phone and put inside your ears to listen to songs so that you do not disturb those around you. These mini speakers can lead to hearing loss if not used at a safe volume.

Listening to music that is too loud causes inner ear damage. Normally, when your body is injured, it attempts to heal itself. This is not the case when it comes to inner ear damage; it never heals. The inner ear continues to worsen. Hearing loss from earbuds and loud music is called noise-induced hearing loss or NIHL for short.

Because the noise-induced hearing loss from earbuds usually occurs gradually, the problem is not even that noticeable to most people until it is too late. Roaring, buzzing, or ringing in your ears after hearing a loud noise or taking out your earbuds can be a sign of hearing loss. Muffled or distorted noises can also be a sign. If you believe there is something seriously wrong with your hearing, you should contact your doctor. The doctor may examine you briefly and send you to an audiologist for further tests on your hearing and to see how much it has been affected. The audiologist can answer your questions about any hearing loss and how to protect your hearing in the future.

Noise-induced hearing loss from earbuds is preventable as long as you know how to correctly use your earbuds. The louder the volume, the faster the hearing loss, so most doctors will recommend the 60% for 60-minutes rule. This means that the highest volume you should listen to your music is sixty percent, and the longest you should listen using your earbuds at one time is sixty minutes. Also, ask people sitting near you if they can hear your music when you are wearing your earbuds. If they can, it means your hearing is being damaged, and you should turn down the volume. Remember, hearing loss can be a major problem, but it is preventable as long as you know the limitations and guidelines.

The following pages have questions based on the texts from Unit 15. You may look at the stories to help answer any questions. Use the back of the page if you need extra space for writing your answers.

1 Which is an antonym for the word *preventable* as it is used in the following sentence?

Noise-induced hearing loss from earbuds is preventable as long as you know how to correctly use your earbuds.

ⓐ avoidable

ⓑ stoppable

ⓒ unnecessary

ⓓ inevitable

2 Luke's hearing was damaged from _____.

ⓐ listening to his music too loudly

ⓑ playing video games with the volume up

ⓒ a loud noise from outside

ⓓ Cal shouting

3 What were two signs that Luke's hearing was damaged?

a. _____

b. _____

4 Which sentences from the text helped you to answer #3?

_____

_____

_____

5 List two facts from the text "Hearing Loss from Earbuds."

a. _____

_____

b. _____

_____

6 Write a persuasive sentence to convince someone to stop listening to loud music through his or her earbuds.

_____

_____

_____

_____

7 What are two things you can do to help prevent noise-induced hearing loss?

_____

_____

_____

_____

8 Which of these symptoms is not a sign of hearing loss?

(a) ringing in the ears

(b) muffled noises or hearing

(c) pounding headaches after hearing loud noises

(d) a roaring sound after hearing loud noises

9 What is true about Cal?

(a) He is a selfless friend.

(b) He doesn't care about Luke's hearing.

(c) He is frustrated with Luke.

(d) He is happy that he can play video games without Luke.

10 A doctor will send you to a(n) _____ if your hearing needs further testing.

(a) dermatologist

(b) audiologist

(c) inner-hearing surgeon

(d) ear-canal specialist

Time to Write!

Directions: Imagine that your friend is listening to loud music and won't turn it down. Write a speech to convince him or her to turn down the music and protect his or her hearing.

_____

_____

_____

_____

_____

_____

_____

_____

_____

_____

_____

_____

_____

_____

_____

_____

_____

_____

_____

_____

_____

_____

_____

Marco? Polo!

Ben could not find his sister or his mother. He knew they couldn't be too far away, but the superstore where they were shopping for groceries felt colossal compared to the small, local grocery store where they normally shopped. Ben imagined if they stayed at this store for very long, they would need two or three grocery carts to get everything out to their car. Of course, right now, that was the least of his problems. He needed to find his mother and his sister before he started worrying about how they were going to get so many groceries back to their house.

As Ben looked down the first two aisles he passed, he saw no sign of his family. He couldn't believe how quickly he'd lost sight of them! One minute they were all together, and then he'd bent down to tie his shoelace. When he'd looked up, he was the only person still standing in the aisle. If only he had a phone, he could call his mother, so he could find out where she went. With no phone and no idea where his family had gone, he wasn't quite sure what to do. Ben looked down two more aisles before moving to stand beside a kiosk where refreshments were being sold. As he stood there, he suddenly heard a voice.

"Marco?" Ben strained to hear where the sound had come from. He knew that voice. It was his sister.

"Marco?" the voice said again. Ben grinned. This time, he was sure it was his sister. He hollered back, "Polo!"

Ben began to move toward the sound of his sister's voice as she continued to call out the word *Marco*, and he answered her back each time. It didn't take long before his mother and sister found him.

"Oh, Ben!" His mother cried as she gave him a big hug. "Don't scare me like that again. If your sister hadn't come up with the idea to play the same hide-and-seek game you two play when you are out in the pool, we might still be looking for you. I'm glad you weren't too shy to answer her each time." Ben totally agreed. He knew Marco Polo had lived long ago, but today, the famous explorer had been a big help to him and his family!

Marco Polo was born in 1254 and died in 1324. He was a merchant who lived with his family in the Italian city of Venice. Marco Polo, however, is not famous for his occupation. He is best known because of a book he helped write about his travels and explorations during the time he lived in Asia under the rule of Kublai Khan.

When Marco was seventeen years old, he set out on a journey with his father and uncle. They traveled on a popular trade route that was known later as the Silk Road. They were headed to China. The ruler of the Mongolian Empire, Khan, took an instant interest in the seventeen-year-old merchant. He gave Marco a position in his court to help conduct official business, such as collecting taxes. His father and uncle were also assigned tasks to conduct. Unable to simply leave, they needed permission from Khan to be able to go. After many years, he asked the Polo family to escort a princess to her soon-to-be husband who was located in Persia. The trip to Persia took eighteen months. When they arrived, they discovered the man who was to marry the princess was, in fact, dead. They stayed for nine months until another husband was found for the princess. From Persia, they began their travel home. They finally arrived home in Venice in 1295.

After their return home, Marco Polo became a prisoner of war. During the time he was held captive, he met a well-known writer of the time. The two collaborated and wrote about Marco's travels and adventures during his time in Asia. The book, which was titled *The Travels of Marco Polo*, later became known by the simple title, *The Travels*. In the book, Marco told about many things that the people of Europe had never seen or heard of before. He wrote about Khan's many palaces, coal and how it burned, eyeglasses that helped people to see, and the Mongolian's postal service. Marco would eventually be released from prison, and people everywhere would read the book that was written during the time he was incarcerated. Many people refused to believe what he wrote, but to others, his words were inspirational. Even Christopher Columbus is said to have carried Marco's book with him as he set out on his famous exploration.

The following pages have questions based on the texts from Unit 16. You may look at the stories to help answer any questions. Use the back of the page if you need extra space for writing your answers.

1 What problem does Ben have?

ⓐ He does not know how to tie his shoe.

ⓑ He has forgotten to bring money to the store.

ⓒ He does not know how to play the hide-and-seek game his sister is playing.

ⓓ He has lost his mother and sister.

2 How is Ben able to find his family?

ⓐ He asks people in the store to help him look.

ⓑ He hears his sister's voice.

ⓒ He knows a lot of information about the life of the explorer Marco Polo.

ⓓ He finds his mother first, and she helps him find his sister.

3 Write one way Marco Polo and Ben are similar.

_____

_____

4 Explain why the text about Marco Polo is titled "Travels."

_____

_____

_____

5 List in chronological order three events that happened in the text "Marco? Polo!"

a. _____

_____

b. _____

_____

c. _____

_____

6 Who else traveled with Marco Polo on his adventures?

     (a) Khan and his father

     (b) his father and his uncle

     (c) his wife and his father

     (d) no one

7 Which famous explorer was inspired by Marco Polo's book?

_____

8 Write the sentence(s) from the text that helped you to answer #7.

_____

_____

_____

_____

9 What does the word *kiosk* mean as it is used in the following sentence?

Ben looked down two more aisles before moving to stand beside a kiosk where refreshments were being sold.

_____

_____

_____

10 Ben is scared when he cannot find his mother or sister. Write about a time you were scared, and explain what happened.

_____

_____

_____

_____

_____

Time to Write!

Directions: Marco Polo and Christopher Columbus lived in different times, but both men were brave explorers. Imagine that you, too, are a brave explorer. Write a story about an exploration in which you were the leader of the trip. Describe the many things you see on the journey. Write about who your companions are. Tell where you went, and explain how you got there. Be sure to include all the many wonderful things you see as you go on your journey.

_____

_____

_____

_____

_____

_____

_____

_____

_____

_____

_____

_____

_____

_____

_____

_____

_____

_____

_____

_____

Safe Surfing

Aaron sat down at his computer to finish his homework. His essay for his language arts teacher was due tomorrow. He had started on the essay at school, but he had not been able to finish. He knew it would take him at least another hour before he was done. As Aaron began to type in the command that would bring up his half-finished paper, he decided to check his email before he began the work he needed to do on his essay. He quickly typed in the username and password. Then he scrolled through the mail he had received. Scanning his inbox, he realized that most of the items were things that he could quickly delete. Then one new email caught his eye. The sender told Aaron he had won some money, but it did not state the amount he had won. Aaron had no idea how he could have won anything. He was, however, saving his money to buy a new phone. Maybe he had won enough money that he could get the phone over the weekend.

Aaron opened the email and quickly scanned the contents of the letter. The sender said that he had won one hundred dollars. That was exactly the amount he needed to get his new phone! He continued to read the details about what he needed to do to claim his prize money. Aaron could not believe his luck. He didn't even remember signing up for any contests. Aaron looked at the form and knew most of the answers. The person wanted his name, his address, and his birthday. Aaron could complete all of those by himself. What he didn't have was a credit card number. The letter requested that he provide the number for a credit card before he could claim his prize money.

Just then, Aaron heard the front door open and knew his mother was home. He called her into the room and told her his great news. She leaned over him and began reading the screen. Aaron watched her face form a frown as she read the information on the screen.

"Aaron, she began, "you cannot complete this form, and you should never give personal information out to an unknown source in cyberspace. This is not a legitimate site. It was good that you asked me to read it first, but you have to be smart whenever you are on the computer."

Aaron knew his mother was right. They had studied about the possible dangers of cyberspace at school. He knew he wasn't going to get any money, but he could at least get an A on his paper!

The invention of the Internet cannot be accredited to only one person. Many scientists worked to create the vast system we have now. However, the World Wide Web as we now know it can be attributed to the scientist Tim Berners-Lee. The Web is the means by which we usually access online materials people use today. Once the Internet became something people other than scientists could use, the amount of information that could be shared surpassed everyone's expectations. The world suddenly became smaller as everyone became connected.

With nearly instant accessibility to people all over the world, children using computers must be especially cognizant of what is happening on the Web. They must realize that there is both appropriate and inappropriate information at their fingertips. They must also be aware that not everything that comes into their homes via their computers is always good. Sadly, many children forget that someone they meet on the computer is still a stranger. All of the rules a child learns about communicating with strangers still apply. Too many children believe everything they read or see on the Internet.

How can people protect themselves out in cyberspace? Be smart about what you're doing while you're on the Internet. Be sure to know and follow a few simple rules to keep yourself safe. Never communicate with strangers when you are online. If a stranger tries to communicate with you online, even if you are ignoring them, tell an adult. He or she will always help you. Don't forget to let your parents know, too. They want to know, so they can help keep you safe! Only join a club or other contests online if you have your parents' permission. Many of these sites ask for personal information, such as your address and phone number. These should never be given out unless you have approval from your parents.

Being out on the World Wide Web is a great thing, but remember to be smart when you are surfing the Web. Cyberspace is a big place. You don't ever want to get lost while you're there!

UNIT 17 QUESTIONS

Name _____ **Date** _____

The following pages have questions based on the texts from Unit 17. You may look at the stories to help answer any questions. Use the back of the page if you need extra space for writing your answers.

1 Why is Aaron excited about the email he sees?

  (a) He has an email from a celebrity he has recently written.

  (b) He has an email response from a game store he has written.

  (c) He has an email that asks for him to donate money.

  (d) He has an email that says he has won some money.

2 What is Aaron trying to buy with the money he has saved?

  (a) a bicycle

  (b) a computer

  (c) a game system

  (d) a phone

3 Write the sentence(s) from the text that helped you to answer #2.

_____

_____

_____

4 What does the word *cognizant* mean as it is used in the following sentence?

Children using computers must be especially cognizant of what is happening on the Web.

_____

_____

5 List in chronological order three events that happened in the text "Safe Surfing."

  a. _____

_____

  b. _____

_____

  c. _____

_____

6 Which is a synonym for the word *vast* as it is used in the following sentence?

Many scientists worked to create the vast system we have now.

    (a) average

    (b) miniscule

    (c) immense

    (d) unusual

7 Why is Aaron unable to complete the form that is sent to him?

    (a) He does not know his address.

    (b) He does not have a credit card number.

    (c) He does not know the year he was born.

    (d) He does not know how to write a response.

8 Explain how not knowing the answer to a question ended up being a good thing for Aaron.

_____

_____

_____

9 What do the two texts have in common?

_____

_____

_____

_____

10 Based on information from the text, which statement is not true?

    (a) Children must be aware that not everything that comes into their homes via their computers is always good.

    (b) Many children forget that someone they meet on the computer is still a stranger.

    (c) Everyone a child meets on the computer is a friend.

    (d) People can access online materials using the Web.

Time to Write!

Directions: Write a safety bulletin for students to read that will remind them to be safe while surfing the Web. Use all the information you have gained from reading the two texts to help you write your important announcement. Fill in each space with safety tips and information.

Safety in Cyberspace

A Safety Bulletin with Safety Tips for Using the World Wide Web

Family Leaders

Scott got off the bus and ran into the house. He could not wait to call his father and tell him his good news. For the past month, Scott had been working tirelessly on his campaign to become president of his class at school. His father had helped him make posters for his campaign and had helped him print flyers to pass out at school. Scott's father had listened attentively as Scott had talked about the improvements he hoped he could make at his school if he were elected as president. The election had been held that day, and Scott had received the news that he won!

Once he was inside the front door, he dropped his backpack on the table in the entry hall. Then he ran up the stairs to his room to find his phone so he could call his father. He listened to the sound of the rings on the other line before it was finally answered. His father's secretary's voice came across the line informing Scott that his father was in a meeting but that she would have him call Scott the minute the meeting was over. Scott assured her it was not an emergency. He told her he would wait for his father to arrive home, and he would simply talk to him then.

Wondering what to do to fill the time until his father's arrival, Scott decided to begin working on some of the campaign promises he had made to his class. He pulled out his computer and began writing letters to the principal about one of the issues he hoped to improve. Many of the students had agreed with him that the school buses were too crowded. He decided to start with this problem. He began composing his letter, listing specific facts and information he had gathered about the problem during the time of his campaign. He had not wanted to be a class president who made promises he couldn't keep. Scott had been very careful to only talk about things he thought he might be able to change, so people could trust him to do the right thing. He was just writing the final paragraph of his letter when his father came through the front door. Scott jumped up to meet him and tell him the good news.

"I'm so proud of you, son," his father said. "I knew you could do it. I think we should go out to eat and celebrate."

"I couldn't have done it without you," Scott told his father.

"Did I ever tell you I was the president of my class?" his father asked Scott.

"Wow!" Scott exclaimed. "Two presidents in one family. That gives us even more reason to celebrate!"

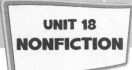

A Special Bond

George H.W. Bush became the forty-first president of the United States in 1989. He served as president until 1993. His son, George W. Bush, also became the president of the United States. He took over the office in 2001. He became the first son to follow his father into the office since 1825. John Quincy Adams was the sixth president of the United States, and he followed his own father, John Adams, who was the second president.

George H.W. Bush was the son of a United States senator. He was born on June 12, 1924 in Massachusetts. He went into the military after graduating from high school. He became the Navy's youngest pilot to fly at that time. In World War II, his plane was hit during a bombing run on the Pacific. He managed to escape his burning aircraft and was rescued by the Navy. He was awarded the Distinguished Flying Cross for the service he gave his country during World War II. Eventually, he became involved in politics. He became vice president to Ronald Reagan in 1980 and served with him for the eight years that Reagan was president. After Reagan's departure, Bush took his place as president.

George W. Bush was born July 6, 1946 in Connecticut. He became the 43rd president of the United States. He is the oldest child of George H.W. and Barbara Bush. The younger Bush became deeply involved in politics as he helped his father with his campaign. He later ran for governor of Texas. He won the election and became the first child of a United States president to be elected as governor of a state. In 2001, he became the president of the United States. He held office during the attacks on the United States on September 11 and led the country's response during these tumultuous times.

George H.W. Bush and George W. Bush will always have a unique place in American history. Only once before have both father and son been elected as president of the United States. As the country continues to exist, such a special event could happen again!

The following pages have questions based on the texts from Unit 18. You may look at the stories to help answer any questions. Use the back of the page if you need extra space for writing your answers.

1   Which word best describes the elections that are discussed in the text "A Special Bond"?

    a unique

    b undermined

    c undecided

    d uncertain

2   In which war did George H.W. Bush serve his country?

    a Vietnam War

    b Civil War

    c World War I

    d World War II

3   Write the sentence(s) from the text that helped you to answer #2.

_____

_____

_____

_____

4   What do the two texts have in common?

    a Both are about fathers and sons who attended the same college.

    b Both are about fathers and sons who celebrate their successes.

    c Both are about fathers and sons who were elected as presidents.

    d Both are about fathers and sons who were presidents of the United States.

5   Explain why the text is titled "A Special Bond."

_____

_____

_____

_____

6 Based on the information in the texts, which statement is true?

(a) George H.W. Bush and George W. Bush are the only father and son to have ever been elected as president.

(b) There have been two times in the history of the United States when both father and son have been elected as president.

(c) George H.W. Bush and George W. Bush were both governors of Texas and presidents of the United States.

(d) George W. Bush's brother was also the the president of the United States.

7 Based on what you have read, which word best describes the relationship between Scott and his father?

(a) caring

(b) unconcerned

(c) nonchalant

(d) indifferent

8 List in chronological order three events that happened in the text "Family Leaders."

a. _____

_____

b. _____

_____

c. _____

_____

9 How did Scott's father and George H.W. Bush most likely feel when their sons were elected as presidents?

_____

10 Using information from the text, explain how the reader knows Scott will try to be a good class president.

_____

_____

Time to Write!

Directions: Think about someone with whom you have a lot in common. Maybe you look the same or act the same or enjoy doing the same things. Then follow the directions that are given below.

1. The person I have a lot of things in common with is _____.

2. This person is my _____.

3. We have these three things in common:

   a. _____

   b. _____

   c. _____

4. One thing I wish we had in common is _____
   _____.

5. When I grow up, I **would** or **would not** (circle one) want to be the president of the

   United States because _____

   _____

   _____

   _____.

6. The person I have things in common with would say I **should** or **should not** (circle one) be

   president because _____

   _____

   _____

   _____.

First Day on the Job

Carson was nervous. Today would be his first day at his new job. The neighbors down the street from where he lived had hired him to watch their children two days each week. Carson had wanted a summer job, but he was too young to drive. The job was perfect because he could walk from his house to work, so he did not have to arrange any special transportation. He also liked that he was not working every single day. He could still make money but also have some free time to do things like spend time with his friends or go swimming. Even though there were plenty of great things about the job, he was still nervous. He had plenty of babysitting experience, but all of his experience had been watching people in his own family. This would be the first job in which he was babysitting someone's children who weren't people that lived with him! He really hoped he would do a good job. He knew the first day was important because he only had one shot to make a good first impression.

When Carson reached the front door of the neighbor's house, he rang the doorbell. He could hear the children inside laughing. He hoped that was a good sign. Mrs. Donahue opened the door and smiled at him. "Carson, I'm so glad you're here. The children can't wait to meet you."

Carson walked down the hall and into the kitchen. He was quickly introduced to the two seven-year-old twins, Danielle and David. Danielle smiled and said hello, but David was a little shyer. He waved at Carson but said nothing. Mrs. Donahue showed Carson where all the emergency contact numbers were and gave him a few tips about the twins' schedule before she left.

Carson asked the twins to follow him into the living room. He grabbed the backpack he had brought with him and pulled out a pack of cards. The minute the children saw the game, their eyes lit up. Carson asked if either of them would like to play Old Maid with him. Danielle yelled yes, and Carson was pleased to see that David wanted to play, too. The time flew by, and when Carson looked at the clock, he was surprised. He was no longer nervous, and he felt certain his new job was going to be amazing.

The Art of Babysitting

Babysitting can be a rewarding and fun job. However, working with children requires a personality in which patience is a big factor. A good babysitter must also be organized and aware of everything that is going on at all times. It is important for the children that are being watched to have fun, but the babysitter must also do all he or she can to keep the children safe from harm.

Anyone who wants to start a babysitting service should have some type of plan. You need to have a clear idea of how you will find children to be placed in your care. You also need to know how you will get to and from your jobs. A good place to start looking for a job is with contacts you may have from your school, your family, your friends, or even your church. Just because someone asks you to babysit, the job may not be right for you. If you do not want to change diapers, for example, then you should never accept a babysitting job with younger children. If you only want to babysit near your own home, do not take jobs that are far away from where you live. Be sure to consider all the possibilities before saying yes to any job.

Once you agree to take a babysitting job, you need to behave as a professional. Do not take a babysitting job you cannot keep. Make sure you understand what is expected of you and what your job responsibilities will be for the day. Even simple tasks like preparing meals need to be thought out. Think about safety, and know if you should only use the microwave to heat foods. What about food allergies? Know if the children you are watching have any allergies to foods before you prepare them a lunch, dinner, or snack. Be sure to know what to do in the event of any type of an emergency. One way to avoid some situations that might cause a problem is to have an organized agenda for your time. Have different activities planned to keep the children entertained and following a schedule.

Of course, one of the best ways to be prepared to babysit is to take a babysitting course or even a safety course, if either is available where you live. Even research online can provide valuable information about your potential new job. Remember to do your best and be safe!

UNIT 19 QUESTIONS

Name _____ **Date** _____

The following pages have questions based on the texts from Unit 19. You may look at the stories to help answer any questions. Use the back of the page if you need extra space for writing your answers.

1 Tell about a time you were watched by a babysitter, and describe your babysitter.

_____

_____

_____

_____

2 Choose one of the qualities you listed in #1, and then explain how you know Carson has this quality.

_____

_____

_____

_____

3 According to the text, which statement is not a fact?

   (a) Do not take a babysitting job you cannot keep.

   (b) Babysitting can be a rewarding and fun job.

   (c) You need to have a clear idea of how you will find children to be placed in your care.

   (d) Know if the children you are watching have any allergies to foods before you prepare them a lunch, dinner, or snack.

4 Why is it important for a babysitter to know about food allergies?

   (a) The food the babysitter prepares should be free of any allergens.

   (b) Food allergies can be contagious and spread easily.

   (c) The babysitter should bring special food with him or her when he or she babysits.

   (d) It really isn't important for the babysitter to know about food allergies.

5 What is the meaning of the phrase "lit up" in the following sentence?

The minute the children saw the game, their eyes lit up.

_____

_____

6 Which paragraph in "The Art of Babysitting" best explains the starting plan a babysitter needs to follow?

(a) paragraph 1

(b) paragraph 2

(c) paragraph 3

(d) paragraph 4

7 What does the word *professional* mean as it is used in the following sentence?

Once you agree to take a babysitting job, you need to behave as a professional.

_____

_____

_____

8 Which two qualities would be important for a babysitter to have?

(a) patient and caring

(b) rude and patient

(c) disorganized and caring

(d) fun-loving and carefree

9 Explain why Carson is nervous before he rings the doorbell.

_____

_____

_____

10 Think of a time when you were nervous. Explain what happened and why you were nervous.

_____

_____

_____

_____

Time to Write!

Directions: Young people often have lots of different ideas about what they want to do when they grow up. Their ideas may change many times before they finally decide on the perfect job. Imagine you had to decide right now what the perfect job would be for you. Use the space below to write a story about you and the day you spent at your perfect job.

_____

_____

_____

_____

_____

_____

_____

_____

_____

_____

_____

_____

_____

_____

_____

_____

_____

_____

_____

_____

_____

The Clubhouse

Arsen put the finishing touches on the door of the hideout. He and his friends had been working for weeks on making a clubhouse to meet at after school. His dad had given him permission to build a small place in the woods behind their house. All of the boys who had helped build the clubhouse lived in his neighborhood. Each day, they planned to go home and finish their homework, and then they would meet back together at the clubhouse to spend part of the afternoon gathering for their club meeting. They would vote tomorrow on a name for their club.

"Is anyone there?" Arsen peeked around the corner and saw his dad standing in front of the clubhouse. He was smiling as he looked at what the boys had done.

"I'm here, Dad," Arsen replied. "I was just adding a few last details to the clubhouse."

"You boys have done a fine job building your clubhouse. All of the work you have done reminds me of the early pioneers and how they had to make their homes out of whatever supplies were available to them. You all have made a fun place to hang out, but you haven't hurt any of the land either. That's impressive. I'm glad I gave you boys permission to build your place."

Arsen nodded, understanding what his father was trying to say. He felt the same way. He and his friends had only been able to take supplies from nearby sources, but they had still wanted to make something they could be proud of building. Arsen started thinking about the time his class took a field trip to a nearby pioneer village. The people who worked there had shown everyone in Arsen's class how the pioneers had lived simply and used supplies from the land to build their homes and develop their small settlements. They had little money, and even for those who had more, there was really no place to purchase supplies. Arsen grinned thinking about how he and his friends had all emptied their penny banks trying to scrape up enough change to buy the few supplies they did have to purchase. "Dad," Arsen said, "you've given me the perfect name for our club. I think I'll ask the guys if we can call ourselves 'The Pioneers'!"

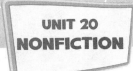
Early Pioneers

When the United States was first stretching out its boundaries, many people volunteered to explore the new lands that were west of the Mississippi River. These brave explorers became known as pioneers. They explored and made homes out of the area that was the American frontier.

In the beginning, many men headed out west to trap furs and set up trading posts. By the late 1700s, many families began to join in the exploration of the new lands. As larger groups began to travel west, the travel was somewhat safer. Larger groups meant more supplies could be carried, and if something went wrong, they might have what they needed to fix a problem. Also, the hostile natives were less of a threat if there were bigger groups to help protect the pioneers from attacks.

Once the pioneers decided on an area they wanted to make as their home, the arduous task of clearing the land became one of their first priorities. Other important matters that had to be taken care of were locating clean water and finding food. Some pioneers used mud and grass to build their homes. These early dwellings were known as *soddies*. Eventually, those pioneers that knew they were going to stay would build more permanent dwellings out of logs.

A child living as a pioneer would begin helping at an early age. Girls and boys would begin working on the farm once they turned ten years old. Girls often learned not only to help on the farm but also how to do all the things that were needed to help run the house. Life as a pioneer was hard, but it was not all work and no fun. Even though many of the settlers lived miles away from one another, they tried to form communities that could work together and solve problems. They would also hold festivals and dances.

Many legendary folk tales exist because of the bravery of the early pioneers. Men like Johnny Appleseed and Davy Crockett were immortalized in texts told by the pioneers.

UNIT 20 QUESTIONS

Name _____ **Date** _____

The following pages have questions based on the texts from Unit 20. You may look at the stories to help answer any questions. Use the back of the page if you need extra space for writing your answers.

1 What does the phrase "stretching out its boundaries" mean as it is used in the following sentence?

When the United States was first stretching out its boundaries, many people volunteered to explore the new lands that were west of the Mississippi River.

   (a) becoming smaller

   (b) staying the same

   (c) moving to Europe

   (d) growing larger

2 Explain why Arsen wants to call his new club "The Pioneers."

_____

_____

_____

3 Why is Arsen's father impressed with the work the boys have done?

   (a) They got the work finished quickly.

   (b) They did the work without arguing with one another.

   (c) They spent very little money to complete the project.

   (d) They used the resources they had and did not destroy any of the area around them.

4 What is a *soddie*?

_____

_____

_____

5 Which paragraph from the text "Early Pioneers" best explains what life was like for a child?

   (a) paragraph 1

   (b) paragraph 2

   (c) paragraph 3

   (d) paragraph 4

6 Based on information from the text, which word best describes the early pioneers?

(a) foolish

(b) impatient

(c) hostile

(d) courageous

7 Write the sentence(s) that helped you to answer #6.

_____

_____

_____

_____

8 List two facts about life as a pioneer.

a. _____

_____

b. _____

_____

9 Compare the astronauts who first went out into space to the pioneers that settled in the West. List two ways they are the same.

a. _____

_____

b. _____

_____

10 Why does Arsen know about life as a pioneer?

(a) He had studied about the life of one of his ancestors who was a pioneer.

(b) He had to do a book report for school on a text about a pioneer.

(c) His class took a field trip to a reenactment of a pioneer settlement.

(d) His father had told him many stories about the early pioneers.

Time to Write!

Directions: Arsen and his friends are gathering together to start a club. Use the space below to start a club of your own; however, do not list any members. Complete the following questions to help get your ideas together.

The name of the club will be _____.

At the club meetings, we will do the following things:

a. _____

_____

b. _____

_____

c. _____

_____

My club will meet at this special place: _____

My club will always try to help others. One thing we will do to help others is _____

_____

_____.

My club's motto or special saying will be _____

_____.

These three adjectives describe the club:

a. _____

b. _____

c. _____

Something Extra: Do you think it is a good idea or a bad idea to have a club that only some people can join? Write about your opinion on the back of the page. Do not use anyone's name when you are writing your opinion paragraph.

Changing Times

The sun was setting as Kara sat out on the terrace with her mother. She could not help but notice how beautiful all the colors were. Her mother told her the sunset the night before had been just as beautiful, but Kara had missed it. After flying all day and then arriving in Hawaii, Kara had not been able to adjust to the change in time zones. She had crawled into her hotel bed the minute after they had unpacked. Tonight, she felt much better, but she still seemed to get hungry when the clock said it wasn't really time for her to eat. She supposed while she was on this trip she would simply have to ignore the clock and let the rumblings of her stomach be her guide.

"What do you think Grandmother and Pa are doing right now?" Kara asked her mother. She knew her grandparents usually went to bed early, but she still wasn't quite certain what time it was at their house.

"I am quite sure they went to bed several hours ago," Kara's mother said. "We do need to call them. You know how much they worry about us when we travel. You will have to remind me that we need to call them in the morning and not once we've settled down for the night. I am quite sure your grandfather would not appreciate a midnight wake-up call."

They both laughed, and Kara could just picture her grandfather trying to answer the phone in the middle of the night. He might be glad to hear from them, but he probably wouldn't be thrilled about being woken up from a sound sleep. The door to the deck slid open, and Kara's father walked out to join them. He had a phone in his hands. "Ladies," he said, addressing them both, "I think this phone call is for both of you." He put the phone on speaker, so they could hear.

As Kara said hello, a voice answered back that she immediately recognized. "Grandmother!" she exclaimed. "Why are you calling us right now? Shouldn't you be asleep?"

The reply that came back was full of laughter. "I decided to stay up and surprise you with my call. Now, tell me all about your wonderful trip!"

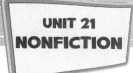
The sun rises, and the sun sets. A day passes in twenty-four hours. Yet, have you ever thought about how time works in relation with the sun and its place on Earth? When morning comes wherever you live, the planet is rotating toward the sun. Midday or noon occurs for most when the sun is straight above Earth. Earth rotates in an easterly direction. This means that the U.S. cities that are on the east coast will see the sun long before the U.S. cities that are on the west coast.

Long ago, people told time by the sun. Because people did not have a fast way to travel or a quick means of communication, letting each place set its own time was not really a problem. However, unsynchronized times did become a problem once the railroads began to travel all across the United States. Trains needed to follow schedules. People needed to know what times they should arrive to catch a train and what time a train would arrive at the station. To help with these problems, the railroad companies decided to set up standard times in the United States and Canada. Eventually, the rest of the world realized the importance of creating time zones as more and more people communicated with and traveled to other countries. In 1864, representatives from many different countries met and established time zones throughout the world. These time zones were based on what time the sun was directly overhead each city. The imaginary lines that run from the North and South Poles and the line known as the equator that runs across the center of Earth were used to set up the twenty-four different time zones.

Because there are so many time zones, when people travel, they often must be reminded to reset their watches. Some electronic clocks automatically reset, making keeping up with the different zones even easier for someone who travels. If you have friends or family who live in different time zones, it is important to remember the time difference when you call them or travel to visit them. Most people like to hear from their friends or family, but they might not be as friendly if you wake them up in the middle of the night!

UNIT 21
QUESTIONS

Name _____ **Date** _____

The following pages have questions based on the texts from Unit 21. You may look at the stories to help answer any questions. Use the back of the page if you need extra space for writing your answers.

1 Why had Kara missed the sunset the first night of their trip?

   (a) She was asleep.

   (b) She was eating her supper.

   (c) She was watching a movie.

   (d) She was sick.

2 What do both texts have in common?

   (a) Both are about different time zones.

   (b) Both are about family vacations.

   (c) Both are about contacting friends and family.

   (d) Both are about the importance of traveling by railroads.

3 What event made people realize they needed to have synchronized times?

_____

_____

4 List in chronological order three events that happened in the text "Changing Times."

   a. _____

      _____

   b. _____

      _____

   c. _____

      _____

5 Why is Kara surprised to hear from her grandmother?

   (a) She did not know her grandmother had her phone number.

   (b) She thought her grandmother would be asleep.

   (c) She did not think she would have a phone signal.

   (d) She thought her grandmother would not call while they were on their trip.

6 What can you infer about Kara's relationship with her grandmother?

(a) They are not very close.

(b) They rarely talk to each other.

(c) They have a close relationship with each other.

(d) They have never spent time away from each other.

7 Write the sentence(s) from the text that helped you to answer #6.

_____

_____

_____

_____

8 What is another name for "midday"?

(a) midnight

(b) dawn

(c) noon

(d) dusk

9 Which statement is not a fact?

(a) A day passes in twenty-four hours.

(b) Earth rotates in an easterly direction.

(c) The U.S. cities that are on the east coast will see the sun long before the U.S. cities that are on the west coast.

(d) Most people like to hear from their friends or family, but they might not be as friendly if you wake them up in the middle of the night!

10 Why does Kara's grandmother think Kara will be surprised by her call?

_____

_____

_____

Time to Write!

Directions: No matter what time zone you live in, there are twenty-four hours in a day. Imagine you could create the perfect day. Use the space below to write a story about your perfect day. What would you do with your twenty-four hours? How would you spend your time? Who would you want to spend time with on your perfect day?

Title: _____

_____

_____

_____

_____

_____

_____

_____

_____

_____

_____

_____

_____

_____

_____

_____

_____

_____

_____

_____

_____

_____

_____

In the Night Sky

Kevin was having a hard time keeping up. The night sky was filled with stars, but it was still hard to see where he was walking without a flashlight. His brother, Brad, had insisted he leave his flashlight back at the camper. They were both attending a star-gazing party that was set up in a field near the campground. Kevin wasn't sure what they would be able to see, but he could not wait to get there. He and Brad had a telescope at their house, but it did not have a very powerful lens. Their father had given them the telescope one year as a gift. They loved looking up at the stars on a clear night. Kevin's favorite thing to watch for was shooting stars.

As the boys arrived at the field, they could already see that many other people had shown up as well. Obviously, they were not the only ones who were anxious to look through the giant telescopes that were set up all around the edges of the field. Kevin saw that none of the other people had brought their flashlights either. He guessed his brother had been right. The only light they needed tonight was the light from the stars in the sky.

Kevin and Brad listened as one of the men invited everyone to view the night sky through his telescope. He explained that all of the people who had brought their telescopes were volunteers. Looking at the night sky was a hobby they enjoyed, and they also enjoyed letting others see the beauty of the universe by looking at the night sky through their powerful telescopes.

Kevin walked up to the man as he motioned for him to join the small group that had gathered around him. He pointed the telescope toward the night sky. Kevin put his eye on the lens and looked up. He could not believe how clear everything was. He listened as the man told him what he was seeing through the lens. He was looking right at Saturn. Kevin stepped away and let his brother look, too. Both brothers had studied Saturn. They knew it had many moons. They knew it was the sixth planet from the sun. Kevin also knew he would have to let everyone else get a chance to look, but he planned to view the amazing planet as many times as he could before the night was over.

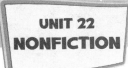
Saturn

Saturn is the sixth planet from the sun. The Romans saw the planet as a golden object in the sky. They named the planet after their god Saturn, who was the god of planting and harvest. Saturn is the farthest planet that humans can see without a telescope, and viewed through the lens of the telescope, the planet is beautiful. Galileo Galilei first saw Saturn through a telescope in the year 1610. His telescope was not powerful enough to see the rings around Saturn, but he could tell that something was there. Eventually, scientists would be able to identify the rings.

In 1973, several centuries after Galileo first viewed Saturn through his telescope, the United States sent an unmanned spacecraft named *Pioneer II* to more closely study Saturn. The spacecraft was able to fly within 13,000 miles of the great planet. Photographs were taken and sent back to Earth. More information was gathered as other space probes were sent out to explore the planet. Today, scientists know much more about the rings around Saturn that make it so unique. The major rings are made up of many closely spaced, smaller rings. Scientists believe there could be as many as 10,000 ringlets! The rings are made up of pieces of ice. Some of the pieces are as small as a grain of sand. Other pieces are colossal in size. The rings around Saturn orbit the planet just as Saturn orbits the sun.

Another unique feature of Saturn is its many moons. Saturn has more than fifty named moons, and there are many others that scientists have only recently discovered. Most of the moons are made of ice and rock. Many of Saturn's moons are round like Earth's moon, but some of the smaller moons are more oval-shaped, like an egg. Some scientists believe these smaller moons may have broken away from some of Saturn's larger moons.

As science continues to advance, people will learn more about Saturn. The planet with the many rings and moons will not be as much of a mystery to those on Earth, but it will remain one of the most beautiful planets in the solar system.

The following pages have questions based on the texts from Unit 22. You may look at the stories to help answer any questions. Use the back of the page if you need extra space for writing your answers.

1 What do the two texts have in common?

_____

_____

_____

_____

_____

2 Why does Kevin say he will want to look through the telescope again?

(a) He wants to view Saturn as much as he can through the powerful telescope.

(b) He wants to move the telescope so he can look at Mars.

(c) He wants to try to take a picture of the planet.

(d) He wants to look through the telescope so his brother cannot have a turn.

3 Which group of people gave the planet Saturn its name?

(a) the Americans

(b) the Greeks

(c) the Romans

(d) the Russians

4 Write the sentence(s) that helped you to answer #3.

_____

_____

_____

5 List two facts from the text about Saturn's rings.

a. _____

_____

b. _____

_____

6 Which statement is not true about Saturn?

(a) Saturn has more than fifty moons.

(b) Saturn's rings are made of ice.

(c) Saturn's rings vary in size.

(d) Saturn has a different sun than planet Earth.

7 How did the *Pioneer II* help scientists learn more about Saturn?

(a) The *Pioneer II* took pictures of Saturn, which were sent back to Earth.

(b) Astronauts were able to land on Saturn.

(c) Robots that were placed on Saturn collected samples to be sent back to Earth.

(d) The *Pioneer II* did not offer any useful information.

8 Rewrite the following statement to make it true: Galileo Galilei first saw Neptune through a telescope in the year 1510.

_____

_____

_____

9 Which is an antonym for the word *colossal* as it is used in the following sentence?

Other pieces are colossal in size.

(a) behemoth

(b) miniscule

(c) enormous

(d) massive

10 Explain why the text is titled "In the Night Sky."

_____

_____

_____

_____

Time to Write!

Directions: There are eight planets in our solar system: Mercury, Venus, Earth, Mars, Jupiter, Saturn, Uranus, and Neptune. Choose one of the planets to research. Then use the space below to write a research paper. Be prepared to share what you have learned with the class.

My Planet: _____

_____

_____

_____

_____

_____

_____

_____

_____

_____

_____

_____

_____

_____

_____

_____

_____

_____

_____

_____

_____

_____

_____

_____

Something Special

"If you are very quiet, I will be able to show you something special." Jacob's father led him down a steep embankment as he spoke. The pace he set was slow, and Jacob was able to keep up easily. He wondered where they were going, but he didn't ask. He wanted to be quiet since his father had asked him to not make any noise.

Jacob tried to step in the same places his father did as he followed him on the trail. He was able to make very little noise as he avoided the branches that were on the trail, and he was careful not to tromp through the leaves that edged the steep path.

Jacob's father stopped walking. He held up his hand to motion for Jacob to stop, too. Jacob noted the trail had come to an end. They stood facing the river. The farm where Jacob's family lived bordered the wide expanse of water. Jacob was never allowed to come this close to the water by himself. He always had fun when his father invited him to walk the property near the water. Once he realized how far they had gone and how close they were to the river, he was certain his father had found something special to show him. The last time they had come down to the river, his father had shown him a giant nest that was the home of two bald eagles. Maybe he was going to show him another nest. He wondered if perhaps the eagles had hatched an egg.

A noise in the water drew Jacob's attention away from the sides of the cliff and down to the water below. His father reached out and touched his arm and then pointed down to the bank. Jacob saw it then. Only a few feet away was a river otter. The otter slid effortlessly through the gentle current. The water rippled as the otter glided by. It was then that Jacob realized there was more than one. The larger otter was followed by two young pups that were obviously her children. Jacob stood beside his own parent and watched as the animals swam and played in the water, giving both Jacob and his father an amazing free show.

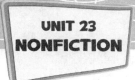
Wet and Wonderful

Everyone knows wild animals can be dangerous, but many of these animals are fascinating to watch as long as you are watching from a safe distance. One such creature is the river otter. This furry creature has a friendly face crowned by small ears and a playful attitude that captures the attention of anyone lucky enough to see one in the wild. The river otter moves through the water with such grace that even the best swimmer is envious. Sadly, trappers have hunted the river otter until many are completely gone from areas they once inhabited. Today, people are working together to help save the river otter from extinction.

Otters live in wet habitats. They are covered in short, dark fur. Their bodies are long and lean, and their torpedo-like shape helps them glide through the water easily. An average otter weighs about twenty pounds. Because otters like the water, they build their homes near large supplies of water, such as streams or rivers. Some river otters have even been found swimming in ocean waters.

A river otter mainly eats fish and other aquatic animals as its food. However, they also hunt animals that are outside the water, such as birds, small rodents, and even rabbits. Unlike some other animals, the river otter does not use its sharp claws to catch its prey. Because they are such amazing predators, few animals bother the river otter. Unfortunately, the young otters known as pups are not so lucky. They must watch out for other predators, such as owls and alligators.

The future for the river otter is looking brighter than it has in the past. Trappers once hunted the otter to near extinction. The otter's fur was valued by many as an ideal material to be used for making coats. Some states have worked diligently to help release more otters back into the wild. This attention to the plight of the river otter has helped keep the river otter safe and sound.

UNIT 23 QUESTIONS

Name _____ **Date** _____

The following pages have questions based on the texts from Unit 23. You may look at the stories to help answer any questions. Use the back of the page if you need extra space for writing your answers.

1 What does Jacob believe his father might show him?

   (a) an eagle's nest

   (b) a school of fish

   (c) a special trail

   (d) a river barge

2 Why does Jacob need to be quiet on the trail?

   (a) His father has a headache.

   (b) His father is very tired.

   (c) His father doesn't want him to scare the animals.

   (d) His father thinks Jacob will hurt his throat by talking too much.

3 What do the two texts have in common?

_____

_____

_____

_____

4 How do you know "Wet and Wonderful" is a nonfiction text?

_____

_____

_____

_____

5 What caused river otters to become nearly extinct?

   (a) They lost much of their habitat.

   (b) They were trapped for their fur.

   (c) There were no pups being born.

   (d) There was no food unaffected by pollution for the river otters to eat.

6 What can the reader infer about the river otter's habitat?

   (a) The river otter must live near water to survive.

   (b) The river otter hibernates each winter.

   (c) The river otter lives in the coldest regions of the world.

   (d) The river otter wants to live in the same territory as alligators.

7 Choose one of the statements in #6 that is not true and turn the sentence into a true statement.

I choose the answer that goes with letter _____.

True statement: _____

_____

8 Based on what you know about the river otter, list two reasons why people would not want this animal to become extinct.

   a. _____

      _____

   b. _____

      _____

9 What type of relationship does Jacob have with his father? Use information from the text to support you answer.

_____

_____

_____

10 Why is the river otter shaped like a torpedo?

   (a) This shape helps it hide from predators.

   (b) This shape helps it swim through debris in the water.

   (c) This shape helps it hide from other river otters.

   (d) This shape helps it glide quickly through the water.

Time to Write!

Directions: Create a dictionary of words and definitions for someone who wants to know more about river otters. Think of at least six words to use in your dictionary. Use the text to help you find words for your dictionary.

> **Example**
>
> habitat: The river otter lives near water, such as rivers or creeks.

Word: _____

Definition: _____

_____

Word: _____

Definition: _____

_____

Word: _____

Definition: _____

_____

Word: _____

Definition: _____

_____

Word: _____

Definition: _____

_____

Word: _____

Definition: _____

_____

The Letter

Manuel ripped open the envelope the minute he found the letter in the mailbox. The letter was from his Uncle Simon, who was in the United States Navy. It was rare that Manuel received a letter from him because he was usually at sea. Manuel scanned the letter quickly as he walked up the driveway and into his house. He could not wait to tell his parents everything that was in the letter.

"Mom! Dad! Come see the letter that came today." Manuel's voice rang through the house. His mother and father were in the living room. They yelled for Manuel to come and join them.

"What does my brother have to say?" Manuel's mother asked him. "Is he coming to visit us soon?"

Manuel passed the letter to his parents. He stood beside the couch, anxiously waiting for them to finish before he began talking again.

His father was the first to break the silence. "Well, it looks like Simon isn't going to be coming to see us very soon."

Manuel couldn't be quiet any longer. "Can you believe he's on a submarine somewhere in the Pacific Ocean? I can't imagine being under the water like that. I wonder if he can see out the window. I wonder if there are any sharks near his submarine. I wonder if he ever feels claustrophobic when he's on the submarine."

"Slow down, Simon," his mother laughed. "That's a lot of questions to ask in one breath!"

Manuel's father motioned for him to join them on the couch. "I have an idea," he said. "Since you seem to have so many questions about submarines, why don't we spend the night looking up everything we can find out about these underwater ships? We can use the Internet to do our research, and if we don't find what we're looking for, then we can head to the library and use the resources they have there."

Manuel liked the idea. He knew he definitely wanted to know as much as he could about submarines and what life must be like for his uncle. The next time his uncle came to visit, Manuel was sure he would have a lot to share with him.

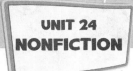

Submarines

Submarines are special watercrafts that can maneuver both on top of the water and underneath the surface. Because submarines can go below the water, they are ideal ships for the military. They are hard to spot from the surface once they are submerged, which makes them an excellent choice for any mission that requires stealth or secrecy. When a submarine is made for the military, it is missing a feature that many other boats have. There are no windows on board. When the boat goes to the top of the water, a sailor can open a special hatch that is on top of the submarine. This hatch allows the sailors to be able to see outside. However, when the submarine is descended below the water's surface, if anyone on the ship wishes to have a view above the water, he or she must use a periscope to look around. The periscope is a long tube that rises up and has mirrors attached to it so anyone who is looking through the periscope can have a clear view of what is going on outside the ship. The periscope is obviously important when a submarine is sent on a military mission.

In 1620, Cornelius Drebbel made the first navigable submarine in history. Of course, his submarine was nothing like the submarines of today. This original underwater ship held only twelve people, and the outside of the vessel was covered in oilskin. To make the submarine move, sailors had to row the ship. It was not until 1775 that David Bushnell made the first submarine to be used by the military.

This submarine could only hold one sailor, and it couldn't dive deep like the submarines of today. Bushnell built his submarine to help the American colonists in the fight against the British during the American Revolutionary War. He wanted to do what he could to help the colonists win.

Over time, submarines improved in both design and effectiveness. In 1864, a submarine used by the Confederates actually sank a Union submarine. By the time World War II occurred in 1939, the United States Navy was using over three hundred submarines to help with its war efforts.

Those sailors who are assigned to ride on submarines know the water is dangerous. Because of the potential danger, sailors are never ordered to serve on a submarine. Sailors that want to ride on a submarine volunteer for this duty. Of course, there is continuous training, and efforts are always made to keep those sailors on board safe and secure as they perform their jobs.

The following pages have questions based on the texts from Unit 24. You may look at the stories to help answer any questions. Use the back of the page if you need extra space for writing your answers.

1 What topic do the two texts have in common?

     (a) World War II

     (b) family letters

     (c) Cornelius Drebbel

     (d) submarines

2 By today's standards, what was unusual about Cornelius Drebbel's submarine?

     (a) The submarine had only one sailor on board.

     (b) The submarine could only go partially underwater.

     (c) The submarine moved by sailors rowing the ship.

     (d) The submarine had one side that was made entirely of glass.

3 Write the sentence(s) from the text that helped you to answer #2.

_____

_____

_____

_____

4 Explain why Manuel is excited to receive a letter from his uncle.

_____

_____

_____

_____

5 Based on what you know from the text, give two examples of how the design of a submarine is different from an above-water ship.

     a. _____

     b. _____

6 What type of relationship does Manuel most likely have with his Uncle Simon?

    (a) They have a close relationship.

    (b) They rarely communicate with each other.

    (c) They do not have any type of relationship.

    (d) They only talk to each other during special holidays.

7 Explain why Manuel's father offers to help him research submarines.

_____

_____

_____

8 Why would the Navy most likely only want volunteers to serve on submarines?

_____

_____

_____

9 Write a sentence that is an opinion about submarines.

_____

_____

_____

10 What does the word *submerged* mean as it is used in the following sentence?

They are hard to spot from the surface once they are submerged, which makes them an excellent choice for any mission that requires stealth or secrecy.

_____

_____

_____

Time to Write!

Directions: Many military men and women would like to receive a letter from someone just like you! In the space below, write a letter to someone in the military thanking them for their service.

Dear _____,

_____

_____

_____

_____

_____

_____

_____

_____

_____

_____

_____

_____

_____

_____

_____

_____

Sincerely,

_____

Living Without

Carla turned on the faucet to her shower. She had been working in the garden all day, helping her mother pull weeds from each row. After a couple hours of work, both Carla and her mother had been more than pleased with their efforts. The garden looked great again. Now all she needed was a shower to wash away the dirt that had attached itself to her instead of staying in the garden where it belonged. Wrapped up in her favorite robe, Carla stood outside the shower waiting for the water to come out of the faucet so she could adjust the temperature, but nothing happened. She turned the knobs on both the hot and cold water, but still there was no water. She couldn't believe it.

Carla met her mother in the hall outside her bedroom. Her mother looked as annoyed as Carla felt. She, too, had been planning to take a nice, long, hot shower. "Your shower doesn't have any water either?" Carla asked her mother, even though she knew the answer.

"I've already called the water company to report the problem. They explained they are working to repair a waterline that is located on our road. They are hoping to have the problem solved within a few hours, but in the meantime, you and I still need to get clean."

Carla was glad her mother knew what the problem was and that it would eventually be solved, but she could not wait a few hours to get clean. She felt hot and sticky. She wanted to wash the dirt off her skin now. Carla looked at her mother as an idea came to her. She saw the slow smile spread across her mother's face as the same idea seemed to come to her. At the same time, they both went back to their rooms. A few minutes later they each emerged wearing their bathing suits. Carla had a bar of soap in her hand and a couple of towels. Her mother had a bottle of shampoo in hers. "Care for a swim?" Carla's mother asked. Carla didn't even bother to answer as she raced ahead of her mother and outside to the kiddie pool.

Water is our most precious natural resource. Without water, life could not be sustained. Our ancestors had to work hard to make sure water was available for use, yet today many people can simply turn on a faucet, and water is immediately available in their homes. Go to any grocery store, and you can buy water in bottles and even gallon-sized containers. So how is all this water so easily available to us today?

Having water to use begins with nature's own unique process known as the water cycle. Precipitation causes water to fall on Earth in various forms, such as rain, snow, and sometimes even sleet or hail. The liquid is collected in many ways. Bodies of water, such as lakes, streams, and rivers, all collect the drops of water that fall to earth. These places become natural reservoirs that hold the water that comes from precipitation. There are also man-made reservoirs that capture water as it falls and help store the water for later use. Of course, not all water goes into a reservoir. Some automatically goes into the ground where it is much needed. Many people have wells to help draw water from below the surface into their homes.

Countries such as the United States have developed water treatment plants to clean the water that is stored in the reservoirs. This treatment removes any trash or dirt from the water. The water treatment also kills germs in the water that could make people sick. The water is then moved into large tanks. A series of pipes that snakes underground carries the water into the homes and businesses that need water. These pipes that are found in your home are called plumbing. This system is a convenience for those who want clean water inside their homes.

UNIT 25 QUESTIONS

Name _____ **Date** _____

The following pages have questions based on the texts from Unit 25. You may look at the stories to help answer any questions. Use the back of the page if you need extra space for writing your answers.

1 Which statement is not a fact?

  (a) Without water, life could not be sustained.

  (b) Water is our most precious natural resource.

  (c) There are also man-made reservoirs that capture water as it falls and help store the water for later use.

  (d) These pipes that are found in your home are called plumbing.

2 In the text "Living Without," what problem does Carla have?

  (a) She cannot get her garden to grow.

  (b) There is not enough rain to make the garden grow.

  (c) She cannot get any water to come out of the faucets inside her home.

  (d) There is a hole in her kiddie pool.

3 Explain why the text is titled "Nature's Gift."

  _____

  _____

  _____

  _____

4 Which is a synonym for the word *sustained* as it is used in the following sentence?

  Without water, life could not be sustained.

  (a) finished

  (b) surrounded

  (c) continued

  (d) withered

5 What solution do Carla and her mother come up with to solve their problem?

  _____

  _____

  _____

6 What are two resources people must have besides water to sustain life? Explain your answers.

a. _____ because _____

_____.

b. _____ because _____

_____.

7 What is a reservoir?

   (a) a place to hold or store something

   (b) a place to shop for specific items

   (c) a place where people who do not have a home stay

   (d) a place where injured animals are rehabilitated

8 Give two reasons from the text why it is important for water to be treated.

a. _____

_____

b. _____

_____

9 Explain how Carla knows her mother has the same idea she has about how to get clean.

_____

_____

_____

10 Think about a time when you didn't have something you needed. Write about what happened and how that made you feel.

_____

_____

_____

Time to Write!

Directions: Water is an important and necessary resource for life to exist. To pay homage to this amazing, natural resource, use the space below to write a shape poem about water. Write the words of your poem inside the drop of water.

Josh could not believe he was sitting in the principal's office. He had only been to this office one other time, and that time he received a special award from the principal. He wished that was the reason he was there now.

The lump forming in his throat made it hard for Josh to swallow. He knew he was in trouble. If only he had not lost his temper at the playground, then none of this would be happening right now. Josh sighed and the slight noise in the silence of the room seemed to finally get the attention of the principal. She looked up from her stack of papers and straight at Josh. She had that look on her face that Josh understood. She was disappointed in him. That look was just as bad as whatever punishment she would decide to give him.

"Well, Josh," Mrs. Fletcher began, "I've been looking over your records for the past few school years, and I can't find a single time in which you've been in this office for any type of disciplinary actions. So, why did you yell at Clarissa until you made the poor child cry so hard that a teacher had to bring her inside?"

Josh squirmed in his seat. He hated that he made her cry. "Well, Mrs. Fletcher, I tried talking to Clarissa first. There was a spider building a web out on the playground. It wasn't near any of the playground equipment. It was right by a group of bushes. The spider was building its web out in nature like a spider should do. Clarissa came over, and she started screaming about how scared she was of spiders. I told her to go somewhere else to play, but she wouldn't. The next thing I know, she's taking a stick and trying to knock down the web. I bet it took hours for that spider to make that web, Mrs. Fletcher. Then, I guess I just lost my temper. I screamed at her. I said things I shouldn't have. She started crying, and that's when Miss Jenkins came over and saw us, and she sent me here to see you."

"Ah," Mrs. Fletcher said. "Well, that makes more sense. So, the web was knocked down and not Clarissa. What you did to protect the spider was noble, Josh, but you don't ever need to lose your temper and yell at another classmate. Get your teacher next time. I will talk to your teacher and explain. You can continue to protect our outdoor friends, but make sure you do so without losing your temper."

Josh smiled with relief. He knew he could handle that!

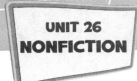
Finding Control

What makes someone lose his or her temper? Why do people get angry? Wouldn't the world be a wonderful place if no one ever got mad? There are many situations and circumstances that can cause someone's temper to flare. Things like stress, personality, and even the changes you are going through as you are growing up could all be culprits in helping someone lose his or her temper. No matter the reason, everyone will get angry at some point. What is important is to learn to control these emotions so they don't get out of control.

One of the best ways a person can control his or her temper is to know what it feels like when he or she is getting upset. Being aware is key to keeping control. Some things a person can do when feelings of anger are just beginning are to count slowly to ten, drink a few sips of water, or try to remove oneself from the upsetting situation.

Another important part of controlling one's temper is having self-control. Many children do not have self-control yet. They have not learned this technique. This is why someone might see a young child throw a tantrum in the middle of the store. As people mature, they are able to control their emotions better; this includes being angry. No one wants to stay like a child and still throw tantrums. However, learning to behave like a mature young person does take practice just like anything else a person wants to be good at doing. For some people, finding control to keep their anger in check does not come as easily as it does for others. These people often need special coping mechanisms to help them. Learning to walk away instead of confronting someone or counting to ten until the person becomes calm again are two things that might work.

Dealing with anger is tough. Learning to think through the consequences of what will happen if someone does lose his or her temper can be a huge help. Also, learning to find other solutions to problems besides losing one's temper and getting angry can make all the difference in the world. Most importantly, remember that anger is a natural emotion that everyone feels at times. It is how a person deals with that anger that makes all the difference.

The following pages have questions based on the texts from Unit 26. You may look at the stories to help answer any questions. Use the back of the page if you need extra space for writing your answers.

1 Why is Josh waiting in the principal's office?

    (a) He is receiving a special award.

    (b) He has missed the bus.

    (c) He needs to call his parents.

    (d) He got in trouble on the playground.

2 Write the sentence(s) from the text that helped you to answer #1.

_____

_____

_____

_____

3 What can one infer about Josh?

    (a) He does not like to get in trouble.

    (b) He cares more about himself than others.

    (c) He believes his teacher is being unfair.

    (d) He is glad he yelled at Clarissa.

4 What do the two texts have in common?

    (a) They are about the importance of a person not losing his or her temper.

    (b) They are about behavior rules for the playground.

    (c) They are about ways to make friends.

    (d) They have nothing in common.

5 Explain why the text is titled "Lost and Found."

_____

_____

_____

_____

6 Think about a situation in which you lost your temper. Based on what you have learned from the text, how might you have handled the situation differently?

_____

_____

_____

_____

7 Which statement is an opinion?

(a) Everyone gets angry at some point.

(b) Stress can cause some people to become angry.

(c) People can learn to control their anger.

(d) Anger is the worst emotion of all.

8 Think about why Josh became angry. Write a scenario for how Josh could have handled the situation instead of the way he did.

_____

_____

_____

_____

9 Which part of the text "Finding Control" best explains why someone might lose his or her temper?

(a) paragraph 1

(b) paragraph 2

(c) paragraph 3

(d) paragraph 4

10 If you were the principal in the text "Lost and Found," how would you have handled the situation between Josh and Clarissa?

_____

_____

_____

_____

Time to Write!

Directions: Everyone gets upset. Most people wish they were better at controlling their tempers. Use the space below to write an advice column offering tips and suggestions to help people control their tempers. Think about your own experiences when you became upset. What were some things that helped you to calm down? What were some things you did that maybe you wish you hadn't done? Draw on both the information from the texts and your own experiences to help you write your column.

Answer Key

Unit 1
1. c
2. Both are about mazes.
3. two of the following: plants, hedges, stones, bricks
4. b
5. a hideous creature; half bull, half man
6. a
7. labyrinth (found in the nonfiction text)
8. b
9. Grant was grinning from ear to ear. It was obvious he was extremely pleased with himself.
10. Answers will vary.

Unit 2
1. b
2. two of the following: hunt buffalo, ride into battle, escape enemies
3. c
4. c
5. noteworthy objects people keep from their past
6. c
7. b
8. a
9.–10. Answers will vary.

Unit 3
1. c
2. Aunt Lindy's husband died while serving his country.
3. a
4. Not everyone may agree that the other holidays are not as special.
5. a
6.–8. Answers will vary.
9. b
10. a

Unit 4
1. Answers will vary.
2. b
3. Answers will vary.
4. two of the following: the crops would not grow, insects became a problem, the dust became unbearable due to the drought
5. c
6. The rain finally came and relieved the drought, and the earth's sighing shows an end to the suffering.
7. Answers will vary.
8. b
9. b
10. Answers will vary.

Unit 5
1. Both are about being fast/speed.
2. d
3. a
4. a
5. Answers will vary.
6. long legs and slender body
7. a
8. b
9. They cannot roar; they do not want to fight.
10. fast

Unit 6
1. Both are about equality in sports.
2. a
3. b
4. Civil Rights Act, women voting, ending slavery
5. This federal change required all schools that received any type of funding from the national government for their sports programs, including universities, to make sure their funds were spent equally on both male and female sports.
6. Answers might include freedom of speech, freedom to practice religion, and freedom of the press.
7. b
8. a trophy with her grandmother's name
9.–10. Answers will vary.

Unit 7
1. a
2. She would want to go because she wants to be a nature photographer.
3. c
4. c
5. Answers will vary.
6. c
7. the tropical rain forest
8. Answers will vary.
9. d
10. a

Unit 8
1. c
2. a
3. b
4. She couldn't help but laugh at how much her mother looked like a tourist as they visited different places all over Massachusetts, but since they were tourists, Karen guessed it was okay.
5. to blame someone for an offense or crime
6. Answers will vary.
7. Karen's mother was a history teacher, and to her, there was nothing more exciting than getting to relive a little bit of America's history.
8. d
9. "I wanted to come here to remind myself that we should expect the best of others rather than the worst. If we believe in other people, they just might surprise us."
10. b

Unit 9
1. b
2. b
3. b
4. Scientists study the areas to help stop environmental problems and to help the animals and their habitats. People from the media film the area to help make others aware of the importance of protecting the land and the animals that live there. Some people are there to drill for resources.
5. Drilling negatively affects the environment where the animals live.
6. Both are about protecting the environment.
7. Answers will vary.
8. a
9. oil spills from tankers carrying the fuel; drilling
10. Answers will vary.

Answer Key (cont.)

Unit 10
1. d
2. Both are about cottonmouth snakes.
3. b
4. c
5. Cottonmouth snakes live in areas such as rivers, lakes, or swamps. They reside near water because their prey lives in the same areas.
6. b
7. The snake is easier to see and avoid.
8. b
9. They are enjoying a final vacation as summer comes to an end.
10. Answers will vary.

Unit 11
1. a
2. Archeologists study the lives of prehistoric people to better understand the culture and lifestyles of those who lived in the past.
3. Answers will vary.
4. a
5. Both are about cleaning.
6. Answers will vary.
7. a
8. b
9.–10. Answers will vary.

Unit 12
1. b
2. Answers will vary.
3. a
4. so they will be safe in the event of an actual fire
5. Answers will vary.
6. This would help everyone know if anyone was still inside the house.
7. b
8. Answers will vary.
9. d
10. Answers will vary.

Unit 13
1. Both are about food allergies.
2. c
3. b
4. a
5. The doctor would watch for a reaction on the skin to see if the patient had an allergy rather than having the patient ingest any of the items that might cause an allergy.
6. b
7. The most serious allergic reactions can cause anaphylaxis. This sudden and severe allergic reaction causes many different symptoms or side effects to happen all at once.
8. Answers will vary.
9. d
10. a

Unit 14
1. b
2. mummies
3. d
4. toilet paper and tape
5. The twins had taken turns wrapping themselves in toilet paper and tape and had even cut little holes out right where their mouths and eyes were.
6. b
7. a
8. b
9. zombie and witch
10. The body was rubbed with oils to stop the skin from cracking.

Unit 15
1. d
2. a
3. ringing in his ears; unable to hear without volume being loud
4.–6. Answers will vary.
7. Listen at a volume no higher than 60%, and listen to music for less than 60 minutes at a time.
8. c
9. c
10. b

Unit 16
1. d
2. b
3. Answers will vary.
4. He traveled to China and Persia. His book is titled *The Travels*.
5. Answers will vary.
6. b
7. Christopher Columbus
8. Even Christopher Columbus is said to have carried Marco's book with him as he set out on his famous exploration.
9. a small booth or section where items are sold
10. Answers will vary.

Unit 17
1. d
2. d
3. He was, however, saving his money to buy a new phone. Maybe he had won enough money that he could get the phone over the weekend.
4. aware of what is going on
5. Answers will vary.
6. c
7. b
8. He did not give out private information to a stranger.
9. Both are about safety in cyberspace.
10. c

Answer Key (cont.)

Unit 18
1. a
2. d
3. In World War II, his plane was hit during a bombing on the Pacific. He was awarded the Distinguished Flying Cross for the service he gave his country during World War II.
4. c
5. The special bond is both father and son being presidents.
6. b
7. a
8. Answers will vary.
9. Answers may vary but should include being proud of their sons.
10. Answers will vary.

Unit 19
1.–2. Answers will vary.
3. b
4. a
5. They were interested or excited.
6. b
7. someone who knows how to do the job and will do it well
8. a
9. He has never taken a babysitting job before.
10. Answers will vary.

Unit 20
1. d
2. He and his friends had built their clubhouse mainly using the materials on hand, as did the pioneers.
3. d
4. A home built mainly out of dirt (mud) and grass that the early pioneers lived in when they moved west.
5. d
6. d
7. These brave explorers became known as pioneers.
8.–9. Answers will vary.
10. c

Unit 21
1. a
2. a
3. the increase in train travel
4. Answers will vary.
5. b
6. c
7. Answers may vary but could include the following sentence: "What do you think Grandmother and Pa are doing right now?" Kara asked her mother. This sentence shows she is thinking about her grandmother even though the family is gone on vacation.
8. c
9. d
10. She knew Kara would think she was asleep because of the time difference.

Unit 22
1. Both are about Saturn.
2. a
3. c
4. The Romans saw the planet as a golden object in the sky. They named the planet after their god Saturn, who was the god of planting and harvest.

5. Answers will vary.
6. d
7. a
8. Galileo Galilei first saw Saturn through a telescope in the year 1610.
9. b
10. The text is about looking at stars in the night sky.

Unit 23
1. a
2. c
3. Both are about river otters.
4. It contains facts about the river otter.
5. b
6. a
7.–9. Answers will vary.
10. d

Unit 24
1. d
2. c
3. To make the submarine move, sailors had to row the ship.
4. It was rare that Manuel received a letter from him because he was usually at sea.
5. Answers will vary.
6. a
7. Because Manuel is interested, his father wants to help him learn about submarines.
8. Being under water is dangerous, and they don't want to force people into dangerous situations.
9. Answers will vary.
10. *Submerged* means to go below the surface of the water.

Unit 25
1. b
2. c
3. Answers will vary.
4. c
5. They decide to use the water in their kiddie pool.
6. Answers will vary.
7. a
8. The treatment removes trash or dirt. The treatment kills germs.
9. She has her bathing suit on and is carrying shampoo.
10. Answers will vary.

Unit 26
1. d
2. He knew he was in trouble. If only he had not lost his temper at the playground, then none of this would be happening right now.
3. a
4. a
5.–6. Answers will vary.
7. d
8. Answers will vary.
9. a
10. Answers will vary.

Meeting Standards

Each passage and activity meets one or more of the following Common Core State Standards © Copyright 2010. National Governors Association Center for Best Practices and Council of Chief State School Officers. All rights reserved. For more information about the Common Core State Standards, go to *http://www.corestandards.org/* or *http://www.teachercreated.com/standards/*.

Reading: Literature	Passages and Activities
Key Ideas and Details	
ELA.RL.6.1: Cite textual evidence to support analysis of what the text says explicitly as well as inferences drawn from the text.	All fiction
Craft and Structure	
ELA.RL.6.4: Determine the meaning of words and phrases as they are used in a text, including figurative and connotative meanings; analyze the impact of a specific word choice on meaning and tone.	All fiction
Range of Reading and Level of Text Complexity	
ELA.RL.6.10: By the end of the year, read and comprehend literature, including stories, dramas, and poems, in the grades 6–8 text complexity band proficiently, with scaffolding as needed at the high end of the range.	All fiction
Reading: Informational Text	**Passages and Activities**
Key Ideas and Details	
ELA.RI.6.1: Cite textual evidence to support analysis of what the text says explicitly as well as inferences drawn from the text.	All nonfiction
Craft and Structure	
ELA.RI.4: Determine the meaning of words and phrases as they are used in a text, including figurative, connotative, and technical meanings.	All nonfiction

Range of Reading and Level of Text Complexity	
ELA.RI.6.10: By the end of the year, read and comprehend literary nonfiction in the grades 6–8 text complexity band proficiently, with scaffolding as needed at the high end of the range.	All nonfiction
Writing	**Passages and Activities**
Text Types and Purposes	
ELA.W.6.1: Write arguments to support claims with clear reasons and relevant evidence.	Unit 6, Unit 10, Unit 15
ELA.W.6.2: Write informative/explanatory texts to examine a topic and convey ideas, concepts, and information through the selection, organization, and analysis of relevant content.	Unit 1, Unit 11, Unit 26
ELA.W.6.3: Write narratives to develop real or imagined experiences or events using effective technique, relevant descriptive details, and well-structured event sequences.	Unit 8, Unit 14, Unit 16, Unit 19, Unit 21
Production and Distribution of Writing	
ELA.W.6.4: Produce clear and coherent writing in which the development, organization, and style are appropriate to task, purpose, and audience.	All units
Research to Build and Present Knowledge	
ELA.W.6.7: Conduct short research projects to answer a question, drawing on several sources and refocusing the inquiry when appropriate.	Unit 3, Unit 7, Unit 22